Social Roots

Social Roots

Why Social Innovations are Creating the Influence Economy

Cindy Gordon, Andrew Weir, and John P. Girard

BEP BUSINESS EXPERT PRESS

First published in 2014 by
Business Expert Press, LLC
222 East 46th Street, New York, NY 10017
www.businessexpertpress.com

ISBN-13: 978-1-60649-928-3 (paperback)
ISBN-13: 978-1-60649-929-0 (e-book)

Business Expert Press Digital and Social Media Marketing and
Advertising Collection

Collection ISSN: 2333-8822 (print)
Collection ISSN: 2333-8830 (electronic)

Cover and interior design by Exeter Premedia Services Private Ltd.,
Chennai, India

First edition: 2014

10 9 8 7 6 5 4 3 2 1

Printed in the United States of America.

Abstract

Social Roots traces the history of a fundamental economic shift that is underway. The shift is rooted in virtualization, a key innovation factor, but when combined with influence networks, the significance becomes transformative. The combined power of these dimensions is creating a new economic paradigm based on return on collaboration metrics rooted in social capital theory.

The genesis of this rich transformation is driven by collaboration and social media approaches that began in 2003. Over the next decade, more social engagement tools were added to the growing arsenal of collaborative platforms, many of which continue to change and evolve today. Independently these companies created new ways to perform individual tasks; collectively they change the way we do business.

And all of this rapid innovation has occurred in a decade. For some it is hard to believe how much the world has changed in just 10 years. *Social Roots* is the story of the near magical transformation, written specifically so we do not forget the significance of this decade of leadership in the influence economy. Many of the stories in the first part of *Social Roots* are about organizations that took the opportunity to experiment and experience the power of social networking approaches to conducting business; and social innovators striving to make the world a better place. Their contributions to creating the influence economy are numerous, and their story of how they achieved success creates a tapestry of insight.

Keywords

analysis, history, learning, prospecting, social media

Contents

Preface

*The learning and knowledge that we have is, at the most, but little
compared with that of which we are ignorant.*

—Plato[1]

I have been working in the fields of innovation, collaboration, and social
media with international clients in diverse industries, such as communications, high tech, media and publishing, and financial services, for over
20 years. What I have learned from the diverse leadership roles, client
projects, and so on is that there are some constant realities in play.

First, innovation excellence is driven by the passion of its leaders and
their tenacity to achieve a vision that stretches everyone's imagination.
The stories in this book are exemplary innovations that have helped shape
our increasingly connected and highly virtualized world. For years, we
have been amassing data and information at an astounding rate. Going
forward over the next 30 years, we will remain focused on collecting, but
value will be concentrated on making meaningful connections.

In the last book I wrote with my coauthors, John and JoAnn Girard,
Business Goes Virtual, we examined the forces at play in collaboration,
social media, and virtual worlds, and examined relevance in relationship
to how organizations are using these new social tools for improving their
business and personal interactions.

Now that a few years have passed, it is increasingly clearer to me that
there are more fundamental economic shifts underway and although
virtualization is a key innovation factor the new glue growth factor is
influence networks. The increasing power they have will further accel-
erate world economic governance metrics to shift from narrow return
on investment (ROI) metrics to more return on collaboration (ROC)
that has roots in social capital theory. Some global players, like IBM,
like to call this return on contribution. No matter which way you cut
it, collaboration is the most significant growth engine driving humanity
forward.

Through our global research on writing this book, as founders and authors, we have collectively learned that reciprocity (giving back) is at the core of collaboration in commercial early stage companies like CoursePeer, Helix Commerce, realSociable and SalesChoice, and with increased trust and aligned purpose, or sense making, innovation and growth elasticity increases.

We call this connected new world order the Influence Economy, a world where who knows who really matters. A world in which we generously share what we know with trusted colleagues to evolve the collective intelligence. Through this connection, trust, and sharing one's influence and value increases more rapidly. The behaviors of hording one's knowledge and know-how, within reason, is passé. Openness and transparency are here to stay and this is not just refreshing; it is germane to healthier growth ecosystem dynamics.

The second thing I have learned is that economic value is increasingly more about managing people as assets. We have learned a great deal since the notion of social capital first appeared. In simple terms, it is the investment in social relations with expected returns. Individuals engage in interactions and networking in order to produce profits. Increasingly, these networks are found via the web in social network channels, like Facebook, Google, LinkedIn, Twitter, and YouTube. New innovators, like CoursePeer, realSociable, and SalesChoice are also paving new interaction pathways into process and workflow intelligence where social is embedded into day-to-day work process interactions.

Trust has shifted to consumers or friends in our networks to help us make informed decisions in life. It is impossible to ignore these channels, and businesses worldwide need to develop smarter strategies to take advantage of the social and influence power of these massive social rooted channels to successfully sell their goods and services and increase their brand reach.

The stories of these early-stage companies and newcomers take the reader through their early pioneering years, adolescent years, and into their growth stage. Each chapter provides rich insights on the founders tribal warfare as told in Blogger and also prevalent in Twitter. These end-to-end connections in these companies have not been told before in an integrated manner, so we are excited to bring this book to fruition. We also discuss the emerging death of television as we know it, as content is viewed more regularly now on YouTube and Netflix than any other form of content distribution means.

As you read this book and enjoy our colorful social stories, it is important to recognize what is really happening. Too many business leaders are still challenging the value of collaboration or social networks and their benefits to businesses. It's time to move forward. Having examined valid research sources over the past 20 years, and continually examining why companies grow to be more successful, we now know without a doubt that this is due to healthier human and social capital foundations. When employees are motivated and involved in collaborative business practices (now framed as collaborative decision making) they perform better and hence customers are served better and in return revenues and profits increase.

In the concluding chapter of this book, we explore in more detail what the influence economy is, why increasing embedded resources in social networks will enhance the outcomes of actions, and what are the implications for not seeding social roots into organizational structures for competitive advantage or frankly, competitive survival. Some of the reasons are more obvious than others, but we do know that the healthier the social roots, the flow of information flows more naturally, which has been proven in social networking science. Also, the health quality of the social ties either strengthen an organization's innovation capabilities or strangle an organization's growth capacity, or weaken human alert systems such that risks or dangers to a business are increasingly more probable.

Social networks that have positive root systems provide opportunities to be assured and recognized of one's worthiness as an individual and a member of a social group sharing similar interests and resources, not only provides emotional support, but also public acknowledgment of one's claim to access certain resources.

With trust moving to friends and families and peer networks, and less confidence in leadership in organizations, executive leaders who want to create the right future organizational models will need to embed carefully collaborative decision making leveraging social and collaborative infrastructure capabilities. Collectively, these approaches will enhance human performance systems to cultivate more open, transparent, trusting, and collaborative cultures.

Many of the stories told in *Social Roots* give organizations the opportunity to experiment and experience the power of social networking approaches to conducting business. This book tells the story of the social innovators striving to make the world a better place. Their contributions to creating our new Influence Economy have been significant, and their stories of how they achieved success create a tapestry of insight to reflect upon and learn from.

We close out the book highlighting some of the up and comers in creating new social root movements and, in time, the light of the Facebooks, Twitters, and even Googles of this world will fade as new market players find innovative wedges to do this all over again. Stories of up and comers include new market players like CoursePeer, realSociable, and SalesChoice.

When IBM coined The Smarter Planet's marketing campaign, their position was brilliant, as increasingly not just everyone is connected, but also everything is connected to everyone. With IBM's early roots in appreciating knowledge flows, and social collaboration, and their continual research in developing products to further advance our collaborative infrastructure, they have created a fertile innovation ground for developing companies, such as Facebook, Twitter, LinkedIn, and so on. It is not uncommon for the early technology visionary pioneers, like IBM and Xerox, to help advance the world's thinking. Innovation that is disruptive more often than not comes from the edges, with new market entrants.

Perhaps the big stretch is on social roots for the universe—as connections, communities will move beyond planet earth, as civilization strives to challenge everything around us. Human beings throughout civilization have valued communities. It is what makes our societies, our businesses, and our communities around us prosperous and healthy. For the first time in human civilization, we are once again seeing a shift from the knowledge economy to the influence economy. As we continue to shift to the power of many versus the power of one, we will need to rethink how to design and develop our intelligent communities around us.

The organizations profiled in *Social Roots* have made a major contribution to helping pave new roads for us. They won't be the last. But their stories need to be appreciated, and most important remembered.

Dr. Cindy Gordom
Lead Author

Acknowledgments

To Andrew Weir, co-author of this venture, who has worked with me on this book for four years. The iterations have been endless, with many cycles of refinements. Your dedication to quality research, and supporting me in life, is a foundation I truly cherish.

I would like to thank John Girard for joining the *Social Roots* team as a co-author. John took on the challenge of bringing together the many ideas that we had developed. Had it not been for his collaborative and editorial skills, we are not sure our dream would have come to fruition.

We also owe a debt to Caren Watts, Pearl Gillespie, Darrin Sand, and Frank Terrell, who were the architects of the chapter on LinkedIn. What started as project in one of John Girard's graduate classes transformed into a very clear, concise, and well-written piece on the power of LinkedIn.

We also thank our business partners for their chapter contributions. Dalia Asterbadi, CEO and Founder, realSociable, who toiled away with me to discuss the changing approaches to selling leveraging social—a special thank you. Also grateful thanks to Marwan and Hadi Aladdin, Co-Founders of CoursePeer, with special recognition also to Michael Thorpe for their collective chapter contributions on Social Learning. These chapter contributions helped round out new emerging social technology innovations shaping our social innovation landscape.

In final recognition, my personal inspiration and fire to innovate is socially rooted in my family, who provide me with a trusted haven to be an entrepreneur, innovator, and futurist to unlock my passion in building innovative companies, writing quality research, and telling stories to help us all recognize the imperative to shift to creating a smarter world. With heartfelt appreciation to my husband, partner and friend, Perry Muhlbier, our precious children, Jessica Muhlbier and Bryce Muhlbier—thank you for your patience with my zany life. Final recognition is for my beloved parents, Norma and Benny Gordon, who lovingly started it all. To each of you, gratitude is simply not enough! To my father who has now left this earth, know there are many more books inside of me, you will never be forgotten.

In closing: Collaboration is core DNA to strengthen our world! Social networks and socially smart organizations will grow. Others that fail to listen and learn will simply perish! *Social Roots* brings tribal perspectives together of successful innovators climb to greatness, sprinkled with new comers who are shining new rays of light to guide others to explore new pathways. What is clear for us as co-authors in writing this book is that the world we know is increasingly social. The opportunity to become smarter with social is rapidly underway. Rather than collecting social patterns, we are now focused on making social connections that truly make a difference. We wrote this book to ensure that today's leaders as well as future generations can learn the story of these early innovators who launched this social evolution.

Dr. Cindy Gordon

CHAPTER 1

Our Social Roots

Facebook was not originally created to be a company. It was built to accomplish a social mission.

—Facebook Founder Mark Zuckerberg[1]

Introduction

Social Roots traces the history of a fundamental economic shift that is underway. The shift is rooted in virtualization, a key innovation factor, but when combined with influence networks, the significance becomes transformative. The combined power of these dimensions is creating a new economic paradigm based on return on collaboration metrics rooted in social capital theory.

The genesis of this rich transformation is driven by collaboration and social media approaches, which really began in 2003 with the launch of Myspace and the acquisition of Blogger by Google. Over the next decade, more social engagement tools were added to the growing arsenal of collaborative platforms, many of which continue to change and evolve today. Platforms like Facebook changed the way we connect with friends and family. Twitter spawned a simplified communication connecting model. LinkedIn allowed us to capitalize on the power of business networks. YouTube, Hulu, and Netflix changed how we view visual media. Blogger and WordPress made us all authors and challenged traditional media. Independently these companies created new ways to perform individual tasks; collectively they change the way we do business.

And all of this rapid innovation has occurred in a decade. For some it is hard to believe how much the world has changed in just 10 years. But many wise sages will be reminded of Bill Gates's axiom, "We always overestimate the change that will occur in the next two years and underestimate the change that will occur in the next ten. Don't let yourself be lulled into inaction."[2] *Social Roots* is the story of the near magical transformation, written specifically so we do not forget the significance of this decade of leadership in the influence economy.

Many of the stories in the first part of *Social Roots* are about organizations that took the opportunity to experiment and experience the power of social networking approaches to conducting business; and social innovators striving to make the world a better place. Their contributions to creating the influence economy are numerous, and their stories of how they achieved success creates a tapestry of insight.

Social Media Giants Growing Up

> Our goal is to instantly connect people everywhere to what is most meaningful to them. For this to happen, freedom of expression is essential . . . We don't always agree with the things people choose to tweet, but we keep the information flowing.
>
> —Twitter Founder Biz Stone[3]

Facebook and Twitter, the social web's most important giants, are poised to direct how the future of the Internet will unfold. If you talk to respective founders Mark Zuckerberg and Biz Stone, they will say that they have already changed the world. The intersection of big business and social is nothing new: collaboration, open source, and connectedness have been cornerstones of the Web 2.0 movement since 2006. However, the past few years have just begun to demonstrate the financial value of social platforms and the global importance of the connectedness they generate. By the end of 2013, Facebook served 1.23 billion active users and had a market capitalization of $134.15 billion. At the same time, Twitter as of 2014 supports over 241 million monthly active users and finds itself immersed in discourse on freedom around the world—Twitter is breaking news faster than traditional media today.

For most companies, ignoring social media is no longer feasible. However, it has not been an easy transition, particularly for traditional media giants, like Viacom and News Corp. Social media giants, particularly those with more public reach, such as Facebook and Twitter, are pieces in a broad political struggle that is unfolding around the world. As traditional content producing companies are attempting to deal with piracy and copyright infringement, they are coming into friction with new forms of social resistance. The pressure, for example, against the Stop Online Piracy Act in the United States at the beginning of 2012 coming from social media giant communities and leaders were evidence of this struggle. Indeed, when word got out in 2012 that Twitter might be censoring posts in some authoritarian states, Twitter founder Biz Stone had to address a growing response claiming that Twitter no longer respected their earlier stated principles of freedom of expression. While traditional media companies are clearly benefiting from the dynamic communication possibilities and long tail distribution of social media, they are also in friction. Even the business leaders are on continuously shifting grounds.

Social media giants themselves are creatures of duality. On one hand, they play to social ideals of connectedness, sharing, and empowerment; whereas on the other, they must generate a profit, satisfy shareholders, and act as the key power brokers that they are today. *Social Roots* highlights the successes and failures of four groundbreaking giants. The following is an overview of some of the major ideas.

Myspace

- Myspace was among the first social networking platform successes that started to change the way we work and play in online conversations.
- User profiles include: personal information, blogs, groups, photos, music, videos, and personalized profile setups. Myspace Music became a crucial platform for both independent and established musicians worldwide.
- During its peak years, Myspace grew at an estimated 230,000 new users daily.
- News Corp acquired Intermix and Myspace in 2005 for $580 million and soon thereafter signed a three-year $900 million advertising contract with Google.
- In early 2007, Myspace revenues were $50 million.

- Myspace began to show signs of trouble in 2008, concurrent with the rising popularity of Facebook and, according to the *Financial Times*, due to tensions between management and the Myspace team. The company began steadily losing money.
- In 2013, Myspace transformed from a social media platform to a music sharing platform; there are currently over 14.2 million artists now using Myspace, with over 42 million songs loaded on the Myspace library.
- As of 2014, there were over 36 million users on Myspace.

Facebook

- A social networking site comprised of personal profiles, notes, groups, photos, videos, mobile tools widget attachments, and the ability for developers to make things for the site.
- It is the most popular social networking site internationally.
- As of January 2014, there were over 1.3 billion active Facebook users, an increase of 22 percent from 2012 to 2014, over 48 percent of the user base log in daily.
- An average of 48 percent of 18- to 34-year-olds check Facebook when they wake up in the morning.
- Over 70 languages are now available on Facebook.
- Over 75 percent of the user population is now outside North America.
- Over 20 million apps are installed on Facebook every day.
- Women over 55 is the fastest growing audience segment.

Twitter

- Twitter is a free microblogging network, comprised of user-generated messages of up to a 140 text-based characters. Through the Twitter website, SMS, or external applications, users can include pictures, links, videos, and user-developed applications in their status updates.
- According to Neilson online, Twitter is the fastest growing site, ballooning from 1 million in June 2008 to 21 million in

June 2009, to over 645 million registered users as of January 2014. Over 135,000 new Twitter users are signing up daily.

- Twitter is growing at a rate of 11 accounts per second, with over 58 million tweets per day.

LinkedIn

- LinkedIn is a social networking website for people in professional occupations.
- LinkedIn became truly global by 2008.
- The LinkedIn Mobile App is compatible with iPhones, iPod touch devices, iPads, Android, BlackBerry and Palm devices, and the HP touchpad.
- LinkedIn paves the way to build prospects by empowering employees to network among a professional social network for business purposes.
- In 2006, LinkedIn increased to 20 million viewers.
- As of March 2014, LinkedIn reports more than 277 million acquired users in more than 200 countries and territories, with over 187 million unique monthly visitors.

These four social networking giants have driven more global connections than any other form of communication experience known to mankind. Their roots have laid a foundation for human civilization to forever stay connected.

Blogging Leaders

Blogging is a cornerstone of Web 2.0 and was one of the first tools that contributed to a shift in how companies and Internet users think about and how they use the Web. Although we discuss Web 2.0 as if it was a new technology, the origins of the shift happened in a very simple piece of coding. What changed was not the Internet itself but our conception of it—as people began to blog, it became clear that the Internet's true power lay not in the ability to broadcast information but in the way it facilitates real-time dialogue enabling frequent communication.

The next two chapters tell the stories of Blogger and WordPress, two major players in the blogging world. Blogger was one of the first social successes to emerge from the Dot Com Bust—indeed, founders Evan Williams and Meg Hourihan are often credited for coining the term *blog*, a much more convenient term than web log. Our chapter on Blogger is a story of both financial and conceptual struggle: It presents a small web company coming to grips with the realization that their simple and free publishing tool is much more successful than their complex software product and facing the reality of running out of funds while their popularity skyrockets. It is a story that is perhaps more relevant than ever, as Blogger founder Evan Williams would go on to cofound social media giant Twitter. The next chapter, on blogging tool WordPress is a much different story: One of a young blogging enthusiast unexpectedly becoming the leader of the open-source blogging movement and community. It also synthesizes some important lessons on innovative structural organization that has allowed WordPress to be a profitable brand, unifying three different organizations and offering a fundamentally free and open source product.

WordPress

- WordPress is an open-source blogging tool and developer community.
- The WordPress trademark is currently owned by WordPress Foundation.
- Closely associated with Automattic Inc., which contributes to WordPress and operates the hosting service WordPress.com (not to be confused with WordPress.org).

Blogger

- A free blog publishing tool that allows multiuser blogs.
- Blogger was developed by Pyra Labs, and bought by Google in 2003.
- Blogger supports Google's AdSense as a way for authors to monetize their blogs.

- Blogger offers author support, for example, allowing users to create group blogs.
- Blogging tips the scale becoming the most optimal way to engage with customers for lead sourcing, everyone now needs a blogging presence on the Web.

Television on Demand

Like self-publishing on blogs, multimedia has been a crucial component of the social web. Blogs, microblogs, and social networks privilege short attention spans, and short striking posts usually make way to longer pieces of content. A 2011 study by S. Adam Brasel and James Gips found that when people sat between two screens, a television and a computer monitor, 78.6 percent of the participants spend more than half of the time looking at the computer, and during that time, attention spans are extremely short.[4] Gazes are being directed away from the television—but not from television content. Video has become just as important a source of information and text: it has been seamlessly embedded across the social web. More than ever, people are accessing television content on the Web just as quickly as they are accessing feature films and noncopyrighted and creative commons content.

The past two years have been particularly contentious with regards to video. The conflict between boundless Internet users and multinational corporations over video sharing is no longer being played out on You-Tube. Media corporations and major video streaming sites —though still in tenuous and experimental territory—have come to settle on somewhat stable ground. YouTube has been embedding ads before videos and record companies are branding the spaces around music videos on the platform. Indeed, the battle over copyrighted content has largely moved to file sharing on cloud spaces—allowing sites like YouTube and Vimeo a strong legitimacy for advertisers and marketing companies.

Video sharing is a very important component to the business applications of social media. Its key applications range from media product distribution to viral video integrated marketing campaigns to HR initiatives and information sharing. The next chapter tells the story of YouTube the first and biggest video sharing sites on the Web.

YouTube

- The Internet's most important video sharing community.
- Focus is on providing an easy interface for viewing and sharing online video content.
- Over 6 billion hours of video watched each month on YouTube.
- More than 1 billion unique users visit YouTube each month.
- One hundred hours of video are uploaded to YouTube every minute.
- Eighty percent of YouTube traffic comes from outside the United States.
- YouTube is localized in 61 countries and across 61 languages.
- According to Nielsen, YouTube reaches more U.S. adults ages 18 to 34 than any cable network.
- Millions of subscriptions happen each day. The number of people subscribing daily is up more than three times since last year, and the number of daily subscriptions is up more than four times since last year.
- Forty percent of YouTube's watching now comes from mobile.

There are other market leaders in video on demand, including Hulu and Netflix that have also made incredible contributions to shaping this market. Hulu, for example, has over 4 million subscribers and Netflix has over 38 percent of North Americans using their service. Each of these video services is rapidly growing, as eyeballs increasingly turn to viewing Internet-based content.

Social Media Trends: What's Next?

The first seven chapters of this book cover the trends in social networking, early blogging innovators, and video social Goliath, YouTube. When we stepped back from our research, it was clear that there were other social trends that needed to be addressed. These trends are changing the social landscape itself, impacting traditional business processes, and bringing return on investment (ROI) back into focus. Our last three chapters on social learning, social prospecting in sales, and social analytics tackle some of these larger trends that are impacting business worldwide.

We take a different approach in these last three chapters, and trace the evolution of market leaders who are shaping these verticalized social innovations. Moving away from the market giants, we highlight diverse companies that have made a contribution to these segments. Some of these are up and comers that we see transforming our social landscape further.

Social Learning

Chapter 9 on Social Learning explores how education has moved beyond formal learning settings. This chapter uncovers the early contributions of chat applications—like ICQ (launched in 1996) and MSN Messenger (launched in 1999)—which staged the evolution for future collaboration tools by allowing users to interact, send files, and store transcripts of conversations. It also highlights the up-and-comer CoursePeer, a company that has combined social media, collaboration, social learning, and also decision-making tools to create highly interactive social learning experiences.

Social Prospecting

Chapter 10, Social Prospecting, focuses on the discipline of sales strategies over the past 100 years and new tools for automating the addition of social information to the mix. We are seeing new companies striving to pull social information from the Web into existing sales tools and processes, allowing sales organizations to identify buying signals that will allow them to connect with customers better and in their preferred channels.

This chapter explores the footprints of the early market leaders, like IBM and Compuserve, with their online discussion boards, highlights Amazon's use of social media to engage their customers, discusses how Eloqua and ReachLocal developed approaches for customer live chat interactions, and profiles a new market player, realSociable.

An example of how social media is mainstreaming into core business processes is realSociable. In this case, realSociable has embedded their application into sales CRM platforms SalesForce and SalesChoice. Uniquely, realSociable integrates social engagement directly into core sales cycle activities from prospecting to full funnel engagement cycle: The application works continually in the background and pulls new social information about prospects and clients and their respective companies. These types of innovative solutions are rounding up amorphous world online social information and turning it into clean actionable insights.

Social Analytics

Chapter 11 examines social analytics and the rise of predictive analytics. The universe of social has created a lot of noise in customer conversation and their interaction patterns. This noise has resulted in a new requirement to do the sense making. There is a persistent set of questions when it comes to social:

- Where are the conversations happening?
- What is happening?
- Is the conversation part of a larger trend? Is the topic trending?
- Which channels are most effective to engage in?
- Most importantly: Where is the propensity to convert to purchasing a product or service? Similarly, where is the propensity to convert to giving information and feedback to support marketing or customer service needs?

In other words, despite all this hoopla about social media, the buck always stops at the question of ROI. This chapter defines *social media analytics*, and the types of questions that social media analytic market leaders are answering via platforms like radian6 (acquired by SalesForce.com) and HootSuite. It also explores the field of predictive analytics, which provide organizations an indication of how patterns are trending and what the statistical odds are of trends impacting business performance or of going viral.

The Internet is so vast and so rich with data from so many different sources that the next big thing unfolding is Big Data and predictive analytics. Before long, social media will be enveloped into mainstream business processes and integrated into how we work. Advanced predictive analytic technologies will be doing sense making on patterns unfolding in real time to inform and alert us. These tools will effectively predict our best future options based on vast amounts of historical data.

The Internet of things is simply getting bigger, and as a result advanced mathematics and advanced scientific approaches are gaining prominence. Companies like SalesChoice Inc., headquartered in Toronto, Canada, have, for example, partnered with the University of Toronto's Big Data and Predictive Analytics Lab to develop an advanced prediction engine to be used by sales professionals to forecast their sales. The patterns going on from all sources, social just being one, will start to create a SalesGPS knowing all the interaction touch points between a customer and a sales or customer service professional.

What's Next

Chapter 12 provides a short conclusion on what's next. We know for certain that what we have unlocked in just 10 years of innovation is nothing in comparison to what the next 10 years will unleash. Our world is getting much smarter and we all need to embrace technology much faster. The agile and speed imperative is now a constant. We can already see evidence everywhere that social interactions are now simply going mainstream into core business processes and practices. One might say social is becoming passé quickly. This last chapter also highlights early insights of Dr. Cindy Gordon's next book, entitled: *The Intelligent Nest: Why Big Data & Predictive Analytics Is the Next Big Thing.*

In closing, we would like to acknowledge Alvin Toffler, one of our world's greatest futurists, as he aptly predicted in *Future Shock* (1970): "The illiterate of the 21st century will not be those who cannot read and write, but those who cannot learn, unlearn, and relearn."[5]

We hope you will enjoy reading this book as much as we have in writing it for you and appreciate that new footsteps are already being imprinted. Respecting the history of these social innovation leaders is important, as their stories and roots have allowed us to modernize how we live, and interact with one another.

CHAPTER 2

Facebook

Founded

February 2004, at Harvard University as thefacebook.com

Founders

Mark Zuckerberg
Dustin Moskovitz
Eduardo Saverin
Andrew McCollum
Chris Hughes

Current Management[1]

Mark Zuckerberg, Founder, Chairman, and Chief Executive Officer
Sheryl Sandberg, Chief Operating Officer
David Ebersman, Chief Financial Officer
Mike Schroepfer, Chief Technology Officer and Vice President of
    Engineering

Overview

Public company traded as NASDAQ: FB
Headquartered in Menlo Park, California
Revenue: $7.87 billion (2013)[2]
Net income: $1.5 billion (2013)[3]
Market capitalization (December 31, 2013): $134.15 billion[4]
Website: www.facebook.com
Alexa Global Rank (February 2014): 2[5]
Members (December 31, 2013): 1.23 billion monthly active users[6]

Timeline

February 2004—Thefacebook.com is launched at Harvard with five cofounders.

March 2004—Expansion to other Ivy League universities.

December 2004—Reaches 1 million users.

May 2005—Raises $12.7 million in venture capital from Accel Partner.

September 2006—Released to anyone with a valid e-mail address.

October 2007—Valued at US$15 billion.

May 2009—Overtakes Myspace in unique visitors.

July 2009—Hits 225 million users.

July 2010—Reaches 500 million users.

July 2011—Hits 750 million users.

February 2012—IPO values the company at approximately $100 billion.

April 2012—Facebook buys Instagram for $1 billion.

September 2013—Facebook reaches 1.19 billion users.

September 2013—507 million users access the platform daily through mobile.

October 2013—Facebook buys Onavo (Mobile Analytics).

January 2014—Facebook hits over 1.27 billion users.

Early Roots

Facebook's roots date back to 2003, when future founder and CEO, Mark Zuckerberg was in his second year of a psychology degree at Harvard University. Zuckerberg, late one fall night in his dorm room, conceived of a school-wide social site that operated along the same lines as Hotornot.com. He envisioned a site on which students could compare friends. The service would place students' photos, taken from the school's online facebooks side by side, and users could then rate which photo was more attractive. It was not long before he successfully created the site and gained instant notoriety because of it. The site was called Facemash and was controversial for two reasons: the first was that many found the site to be simply unethical, as Zuckerberg had posted students' pictures without consent, and the second was that in order to obtain these photos, he had to hack the university's facebook systems. Harvard revoked Zuckerberg's Internet access within hours of the website being online. However, during Facemash's short lifetime, 450 students signed up and logged a total of roughly 2,200 page views.[7] This "debacle," as one student paper called it, gave Zuckerberg the reputation that would ensure that his next project, TheFacebook.com, was an instant success.

In December 2003, the Harvard publication, *The Harvard Crimson* published an article titled "Put Online a Happy Face,"[8] which noted the benefits of a campus-wide electronic facebook (rather than separate, house-specific closed databases), and cited Facemash as proof, despite the site's unsavory nature. The opinion piece addressed privacy concerns and wrote that, "a campus-wide facebook will facilitate the Harvard community with the names and basics of their peers, without worry of opening the site to unsolicited strangers." In another piece, the paper wrote: "much of the trouble surrounding the facemash could have been eliminated if only the site had limited itself to students who uploaded their own photos"[9]. According to Zuckerberg, he was inspired by the Crimson's staff commentary. He said, "I basically took that article . . . and made a site with those exact privacy controls and that was Facebook."[10]

According to the Rolling Stone, Zuckerberg received $1,000 in funding from his dorm suite-mate, Eduargo Saverin, and registered the domain name thefacebook.com in mid-January 2004.[11] On February 4, the site was launched. Within 24 hours of going live, 1,200 Harvard students reportedly joined the online community. After 2 weeks, they had a total of 4,000 signups; 2 weeks later, that number grew to 10,000.[12] Zuckerberg enlisted his two roommates, Dustin Moskovitz and Chris Hughes, to aid in programming and scaling. Soon, Andrew McCullom, a computer science major, joined the team and by March, more than half of the undergraduate population at Harvard was using Facebook. In early March, other Ivy League schools, such as Yale, Stanford, and Columbia, began to show significant interest in the site, and the team worked to create databases and open the site to an exclusive number of universities.[13] On April 13, they filed letters of incorporation.

Immediately following the end of their final sophomore semester, the team moved to a small house in Palo Alto, California to continue working on Facebook. The group spent most nights coding, but nevertheless began organizing parties using their Facebook. They even went so far as to run a zipline from their roof, making for easy access to the pool.[14] Zuckerberg says he was planning on going back to school, but with the continual growth of Facebook, he was yet to finish his degree.

The summer was a very busy and crucial time for Facebook, but was also marked with controversy. For instance, trouble arose when Zuckerberg received a cease and desist letter from ConnectU, a company run by his former classmates Divya Narendra, Cameron Winklevoss, and his twin brother Tyler. Back in January 2003, the three of them enlisted Zuckerberg to write some coding for a social networking site they had called HarvardConnection. While Zuckerberg did some work for them, he never finished what they asked, and instead moved on to create Facebook. In September 2004, HarvardConnection changed their name to ConnectU and filed a lawsuit claiming that, after helping them with their website, Zuckerberg used their source code, business plan, and stalled their development before creating his own version on the site. The lawsuit was finally settled in Zuckerberg's favor in June 2008.

Facebook's next major growth came in September 2004, with the addition of two new features: the Wall and Groups. These features helped increase Facebook's functionality to a level equivalent to the most popular social networking site at the time, Myspace. Around this time, the burgeoning company received its first investment, in the form of US$500,000 in an angel round from investor Peter Thiel, a cofounder of PayPal. Facebook's growth continued steadily; throughout the year it scaled upward by continually adding new college networks. Its user base reached the 1 million milestone by the end of the year.

In May 2005, Facebook had both grown to support more than 800 college networks. At this time, Accel Partners, with whom Peter Thiel is associated, reached out with a $12.7 million investment in Facebook. It was not until August 23, 2005 that Facebook purchased the domain name Facebook.com for $200,000. As the summer ended, two of Facebook's key employees decided it was best to return to Harvard and finish their undergraduate degrees. Chris Hughes and Andrew McCullom went back to Harvard for the 2005 school year. They both continued to work on Facebook in their spare time, although it was not their full-time job any longer.

On September 2, 2005, Zuckerberg launched what he called the next logical thing to do, a separate manifestation of the site aimed at high school students. By the end of 2005, Facebook expanded into Canada, the United Kingdom, Mexico, Puerto Rico, U.S. Virgin Islands, Australia, and New Zealand, and had also added the Facebook Photos feature.

The Facebook Photos feature has since become the number one photo sharing application on the Internet. In 2009, more than 850 million photos were uploaded each month, up from 250 million in 2008.[15] Today that number is much higher. In terms of sheer numbers, Facebook Photos has surpassed every photo-sharing network, including Flickr. To put this in perspective, *The Huffington Post* estimated in August 2011 that 60 billion photos had been posted on Facebook since its launch (compared to 6 billion on Flickr). As of January 2014, the number of photos uploaded on Facebook is over 250 billion, with an average number of 215 photos per user.[16]

One of the most important years for Facebook's growth proved to be 2006. Over the course of the year, the site's popularity exploded and it would emerge as one of the dominant players on the Internet. In April 2006, Facebook had its first speculation based upon its revenue. Facebook was said to be making $1 million a week. Later that month, the company secured another round of funding totaling $ 25 million. The funding was led by Greylock Partners, Mertich Capital Partners, and Peter Thiel. Meritech's managing director, Paul S. Madera noted at the time that, "[Facebook had] been designated by their community as the chosen community portal. This is a company that the entire venture community would love to be a part of."[17] Madera told *The Harvard Crimson* that Meritech was impressed by "Facebook's rapid growth and its potential for further expansion in the coveted college-age market."[18] Shortly after this investment, Zuckerman announced the launch of Facebook Mobile.

Facebook Mobile increased the site's ubiquity 10-fold. Released at the end of April 2006, this feature consists of three applications: Mobile Web, Mobile Uploads, and Mobile Texts. Mobile Web, allows users to surf Facebook from their 3G phones in a way very similar to the normal experience. Following Facebook Mobile Web, the company unveiled Mobile Uploads: a feature allowing users to upload photos and notes from their cell phone to their Facebook profiles. Finally, Mobile Texts added the functionality of sending and receiving text messages through Facebook. In 2011, over 250 million people were accessing Facebook over their mobile phones. As of January 2014 only 3 years later, this number is staggering with over 874 million users and approaching 600 million daily users, with over 41 percent of Facebook's global revenues coming from mobile ($1.6 billion).[19]

In the summer of 2006, Facebook signed a $280 million dollar advertising deal with Microsoft. This came as a surprise to many, who figured that Google would be the most likely partner. The advertising deal was following the massive Google–Myspace advertising deal that took place at the beginning of August of the same year. The Facebook–Microsoft deal was a minority stake that valued the company at $15 billion, giving Microsoft a 2 percent stake. That deal now is reported to be worth $1.3 billion, based on Facebook's 2011 valuation at about $80 billion.[20]

In September of the same year, Facebook made its most major change: it enabled anyone with a valid Internet e-mail address to create an account. This spurred the growth of Facebook's user base far beyond college and university students. In a press release, Zuckerberg announced: "We are expanding to respond to the requests of millions of people who want to be part of Facebook, but haven't been able to until today . . . About one-third of Facebook's college users have already graduated and are now interacting with more people outside of their schools and work environment." Along with this change came additional privacy controls. Nevertheless, a large number of college and university students protested the change. Over the next few years, Facebook, like Myspace before it, experimented with implementing new services, navigation systems, privacy control, and information sharing. Users continued to be very vocal about what they liked and did not like about changes. Other services that Facebook would eventually end included Facebook MarketPlace, a competitor to classifieds sites like Craigslist, and Facebook Deals, a response to deal companies like Groupon.

Just in time for Valentine's Day 2007, Facebook launched a virtual gift shop. All of the members got one free gift, and every other one was $1 after that. After the gift feature was launched, Facebook began creating a new gift every single day. Originally, the proceeds from selling the gifts went to charity, but after the first month, the proceeds turned into another form of revenue for Facebook. Ultimately, as with other application trials, Facebook would close their gift shop in 2010. In a blog post, Facebook Product Manager, or *Product Ninja*, Jared Morgenstern wrote,

> While the ability to give gifts will be gone, I am proud of the impact gifts have had on Facebook. Out of the Gift Shop's *gift credits* came the virtual currency, Facebook Credits that now makes it easier for people to buy premium items across the many games and applications on Facebook. . . . So while we're returning one gift, we're replacing it with another.[21]

The hope was that Facebook Credits would become a stable online currency that users could use to pay for games, apps, and special premium online products. For instance, in September 2011, Facebook promoted, as their "Game of the Week," an online game called Pioneer Trail. "Now you have more room to play Pioneer Trail!" Facebook announced on their Credits page, "Check out the new full screen experience as you tame your homestead and hit the trail. Purchase horseshoes with Facebook Credits to get more energy, animals, and buildings as you head west on the Pioneer Trail." In 2011, the uses for Facebook Credits widened to include Warner Brother's films.

However, as Reuter's columnist Robert Cyran would argue in a 2011 article, Credits did not emerge as an "Internet reserve currency," or a realistic competitor with PayPal. The currency is pegged at 10 credits per dollar, but users cannot "take them out of the Facebook system, exchange them for cash or give them to other users."[22] Cyran also points out that Facebook takes a 30 percent cut of the Credits transaction, compared to PayPal's, which "is in the single digits." It is worth noting, however, that the online gaming company Zynga, which saw a major success with the Facebook game Farmville, "generates most of its revenue through Facebook, and in 2011 was valued at more than $15 billion in gray market trading."[23] However, today, the market value of the company is just $2.34 billion, well below the once much-hyped hopes for the San Francisco-based online gaming company that has seen nothing but troubled times since its IPO. In fact, since its late 2011 public offering, Zynga shares are down close to 70 percent. This just shows the gaming market can be very fickle.[24] In terms, of Facebook, gaming market trends continue to be buoyant. Facebook, for its part, says gaming has never been healthier on its platform. Tera Randall, Facebook's technology communications manager, said game installs are up 75 percent compared in late 2013, compared to a year ago and that more than 250 million Facebook users are currently playing games on the social network each month (compared to 235 million last October).[25]

User Demographics

According to statistics that Facebook released, more than two-thirds of the site's 1.2 billion active users are outside of college, and the fastest growing demographic is 35 years and older. Of those, daily active users passed 728 million on average during September 2013, and the number of monthly active mobile users hit 874 million.[26]

In the years since Facebook first became publically available, user demographics have shifted and widened. The U.S. market remains one of the most concentrated market with 67 percent of the user base from the United States. Facebook today still attracts the young with 83 percent of the users being 18 to 29. The largest growth segment has been the 45- to 54-year-old age segment experiencing 46 percent growth since year-end 2012. Facebook on smartphones now accounts for 66 percent of total social media sharing on iPhones.[27]

The reason for this shift is rooted in the fact that as Facebook has become more accessible; people in the workplace are joining as well as teenagers before they enter college or even high school. Also, the initial group of Facebook users have now graduated, and so they are continuing to use the service as well as spreading it virally into the workplace, thus creating an increase in people older than the typical college-aged crowd. One of the fastest growing groups on Facebook is the baby boomers. Men and women over the age of 55 are is one of the fastest growing segments.

The Developers Platform

The Facebook Platform was officially launched on May 25, 2007; this was almost one year after Facebook allowed developers to start developing applications in August 2006. The Facebook Platform is a way for web developers to create applications with deep integration into Facebook. This is of great advantage to web developers, as it presents access to Facebook's massive user base. Similarly, it is an advantageous situation for Facebook because it opens the potential for immensely popular applications (including games, organizational tools, and integration utilities) to be introduced and interacted with within the Facebook framework.

Facebook applications are made using the Facebook Markup Language, a code similar to HTML, but with limitations ensuring that Facebook has control over the basic look and layout. With the release of the Facebook Platform, Facebook did the exact opposite of what its competitors were doing. While Myspace decided on blocking outside developers' widgets and content, Facebook took advantage of the opportunity and allowed them greater access to Facebook's core features in order to increase Facebook functionality in such a way that Facebook could not do on its own. At the same time, however, they kept every user's profile rigidly structured.

These applications get access to Facebook's immense user base, as well as the ability to spread throughout Facebook virally, or *organically*. Not only is Facebook expanding its features, but it is also trying to become a place where people spend more and more of their time. With the addition of applications to the site, Facebook has become a hub where people spend their time online. In essence, with the Facebook Platform, the site is becoming a social operating system.

Among Facebook applications, many of them have gained major popularity through viral and organic distribution, and also through methods such as Facebook Ads. Many applications have developed revenue models and are making money with their applications, particularly with the roll out of Facebook Credits. The first Facebook Application to be sold to another company was called *Extended Info* and was sold to SideStep for an undisclosed amount. This was followed just a few days later with the acquisition of the app *Favorite Peeps* by Slide, buying for $60,000.[28] An important innovative application affecting the world of work came with the release of CloudCrowd, a Facebook app that distributes pieces of work to Facebook users. A type of paid crowdsourcing, CloudCrowd is an experiment in labor distribution, users sign in to the application and choose tasks to complete, for anywhere from $.10 to $8.00. The type of work ranges from repetitive data work to writing marketing copy. Not surprisingly, CloudCrowd was named one of the most brilliant companies in 2010 by *Entrepreneur* magazine.

In April 2010, Facebook rolled out Social Plugins: the functionality for websites to effectively integrate with Facebook. With social plugins, a website (external to Facebook) can give users the ability to *like* or comment on content on their website through the user's Facebook identity. Websites around the world increasingly are integrating with Facebook to add this functionality, often appearing as a *like* button on their site. According to Facebook, roughly 10,000 sites per day incorporate social buttons.

Facebook is very committed to helping game developers build games that connect players across website and mobile platforms. More than 260 million people are playing games on Facebook each month—a number that continues to rise. One of the fastest growing categories of games on Facebook are the highly sophisticated, 3D games like: Unity, Urban Strike, Deadzone, and Kings Bounty: Legions.

Throughout 2011–2013, the focus for the Facebook development platform remained strong on its open API, supporting games, taking advantage of social plugins, and developing more innovative development approaches, like open graph, which allow people to tell stories, using diverse artifacts. By developing a more open API strategy, Facebook has ignited users to develop over 12 million applications.

Facebook Ads: Pages, Viral Advertising, and Marketing

At the November 2007 Facebook Social Advertising Event in New York, Facebook announced its plans regarding the release of a new advertising system, allowing businesses to target groups of users within Facebook's network. Called Facebook Ads, it is a system that Mark Zuckerberg said would "represent a completely new way of advertising online." The system is comprised of three parts: Facebook Pages, the Facebook Social Ads System, and an interface "to gather insights into people's activity on Facebook that marketers care about" ("Facebook Unveils").

Pages is a feature that allows users to interact with businesses and organizations in a way almost identical to how users interact with each other. In other words, companies can create interactive profiles containing various types of content, including information, applications, audio, and video. Upon the launch of the service, Zuckerberg announced that 100,000 Pages had already been created. Among them were: Coca-Cola, Sony Pictures Entertainment, and Verizon Communications Inc. This channel can be extraordinarily advantageous to companies; not only does it give them access to Facebook's "social graph," but also when people engage with a company's Facebook page, news of the action can spread throughout that user's network of friends and associates by way of a news feed. In terms of interaction, users can become fans of a page, post messages on its wall, and upload photos and videos (if the management of the page enables such features). In a press release, Facebook wrote, "users can become a fan of a business and can share information about that business with their friends and act as a trusted referral." In other words, when users choose to become fans of branded pages, they self-identify with the brand and become word-of-mouth endorsers among their networks.

Companies that create pages and create a network of fans can purchase SocialAds. These are advertisements that can be tailored to a very specific group of users. Users can be targeted by profile keywords (such as interests, favorite movies, etc.), demographics, or even by specific actions on Facebook. For instance, your company could buy ads targeting University Graduates from Toronto, Ontario, between the ages 24 and 40 that are interested in Virtual Worlds. The result is, as Zuckerberg said, a *new form* of hyper-targeted advertising that draws on Facebook users as trusted endorsers.

A new feature was created in May 2008 for businesses, called Facebook Connect. This feature, now called Facebook Open Graph, allows users to login to their party sites through Facebook. The result is that information flows both ways. While privacy settings changes the extent of information that each user shares with third-party websites, this information sharing gives those sites unprecedented detail in their metrics; their visitors now have names, genders, ages, and friends. Users have the option to share any action they take on the third-party site with their Facebook friends through News Feed. On one level, this is important because on Facebook Pages, the user acts as a trusted evangelist for the brand. But the real significance lies in the incredibly detailed and complex user behavior models that Facebook, and to a lesser degree third-party sites, can generate from these data streams. In 2010, over 250,000 websites had integrated with Facebook. As of January 2014, Facebook reported the number of integrated websites and applications to be integrated with Facebook to be over 7 million, with 20 million apps being installed daily on Facebook.[29]

Fickle Teenagers Challenge Facebook's Future

There are some very new trends a foot which are showing some erosion in Facebook usage among teens. A study by Global Web Index researched Facebook usage among teens. Select highlights from this research is summarized as follows:

- Fifty-six percent decline in usage in the third quarter of 2013.
- Shift in usage going to mobile chat service channels, like WeChat.
- WeChat has seen the most rapid growth in active users aged between 16 and 19 with a 1,021 percent growth.
- Twitter's video sharing app, Vine has climbed to a 639 percent increase from the year prior.
- Flickr has also seen a 254 percent increase in teen usage.
- Instagram has seen an 85 percent increase in teen usage in 2013.
- Facebook's photo sharing market share Snapchat is also growing with 10 percent of teens globally using the service, making it bigger than Pinterest, Vine, WeChat, and LinkedIn.[30]

In summary, the social media landscape is currently saturated with the next big thing. Young people are fickle and easily switch from one social media app to another. While teens leave Facebook and Twitter in favor of newer apps and sites that offer a safe haven from watchful parents, the next great thing is likely just launching tomorrow.

However, irrespective of these emerging new developments, Facebook will simply have to pony up to acquire these new market players, as they have done in the past to keep a leading position in the market place, with wise investments like Instagram, or its many mobile analytic recent purchases.

Summary

Zuckerberg's vision for Facebook is that it will ultimately become the standard online communication platform. "Your Facebook ID," he muses, "will quite simply be your gateway to the digital world."[31] The development of social buttons was a step in this direction, allowing users to access other sites using their Facebook ID. Facebook recently moved another step closer to their goal, by allowing users to choose if they want their network open to the public. The company is continuously developing new ways to monetize their business to ensure they will still be alive to achieve their ambitious goal. There is no doubt that Facebook is succeeding in encouraging people to change the way they live their social lives. Indeed, Facebook has facilitated the integration of social web applications into the daily lives of millions of people around the world.

Today, Facebook is valued at an astonishing $100 billion. This has a lot of people wondering where all of this is heading. Is this overvaluation, seen in other companies, like Skype, Zinga, and LinkedIn, symptomatic of a new tech bubble? In the summer of 2011, Fortune remarked that the analogies to the dot com bubble burst cannot be ignored. However, unlike dot coms, Facebook has embedded itself deeply into the lives and interactions of millions around the world. An important point to take away is that this embedding has wreaked havoc on how we understand value. Facebook has done something incredible; its implications will be long lasting and its value is unprecedented. How we understand that value is a much more difficult question open to interpretation.

What is going to be imperative, however, is for Facebook to keep a watchful eye on where their audience(s) are trending on new usage patterns, in particular with the fickle teenager crowd. Social networking market leader, Facebook, cannot be complacent, and must constantly be on the lookout to acquire, invest, or partner with new disruptive social innovations to either augment or extend their capabilities or create new markets.

As one of the wealthiest leaders in business, Zuckerberg appears to be skilled at connecting with a wide range of people and balances openness, informality with a good bit of nerdy quirkiness with structure and ambition. He has said in the past that he is "here to build something for the long term." He wisely rejected Yahoo's offer to buy Facebook for $1 billion in 2006. At the time, many commentators thought he should have accepted what appeared to be a generous offer in a volatile market and tough climate. But Zuckerberg retained his longer-term focus saying, "we really just believe in what we're doing." At the heart of Facebook is a simple concept: connecting people and empowering them to share the things they want to. Facebook's mission is to "make the world more open and connected."[32] This appears to be Zuckerberg's leadership philosophy. As a young CEO still, will he stand the test of time? With strong leadership around him, and a strong vision for the long term, he has the opportunity to go the long haul.

Discovery Questions

1. What are your perspectives of the court ruling clearing Zuckerberg innocent in the ConnectU case on intellectual property? Should there have been some compensation? What do early stage companies need to do to protect themselves? What lessons can be learned from this case?

2. What is the future of Facebook? Will it decline in brand loyalty to Twitter as it expands its footprint? What are implications of new chat sites like SnapChat, or WeChat in moving traffic off of Facebook?

3. What would it take for Facebook to become the next Myspace? Is this a risk?

4. What is so sticky and attractive about Facebook that will make it harder to switch off?

5. What is Zuckerberg's leadership style, and why will it be important to stay increasingly connected to his talent, as he continues to build Facebook's future?

CHAPTER 3

Twitter

Founded

March 2006, at Odeo Inc.

Founders

Jack Dorsey
Noah Glass
Evan Williams
Biz Stone

Current Management[1]

Dick Costolo, Chief Executive Officer
Ali Rowghani, Chief Operating Officer
Mike Gupta, Chief Financial Officer
Adam Bain, President of Global Revenue
Adam Messinger, Chief Technology Officer
Vijaya Gadde, General Counsel
Colin Crowell, Vice President, Global Public Policy
Chris Fry, Senior Vice President of Engineering
Gabriel Stricker, Vice President of Marketing and Communications
Kevin Weil, Vice President of Revenue Products

Overview

Public company traded as NYSE:TWTR
Headquartered in San Francisco, California
Revenue: $664.89 million (2013)[2]
Net income: $511.47 million (2013)[3]

Market capitalization (December 31, 2013): $34.67 billion[4]
Website: www.twitter.com
Alexa Global Rank (February 7, 2014): 11[5]
Members (December 31, 2013): 241 million monthly active users[6]

Timeline

March 2006—First Tweet sent on March 21.
April 2007—Twitter Inc. is spun off from Obvious Corp.
August 2007—Hashtag (#) debuts on Twitter.
January 2009—First photo from U.S. Airways crash in New York city
    sent by Twitter.
April 2010—Promoted tweets launched.
October 2010—Dick Costolo becomes CEO.
March 2011—Achieves milestone of 1 billion tweets per week.
May 2011—Acquires TweetDeck.
September 2011—Achieves milestone of 100 million active users.
November 2012—President Obama announces win with a tweet.
January 2013—Launches Vine.
August 2013—Achieves milestone of 500 million tweets per day.
September 2013—Announces initial public offering.

Early Roots

From its roots as the hyped start-up in 2008 among consumers, businesses, and technology professionals, Twitter has rapidly become one of
the most important social media services on the Internet. It has a simple
interface and a straightforward concept: a service for users to broadcast-
ing their thoughts to a list of followers in 140 characters or less. Twitter
has facilitated a new turn in media, communications, and user-generated
innovation. On Twitter, individuals Tweet and Retweet to lists of followers and also often to the world at large. In January 2011, it reached a
valuation of $4 billion.[7] As of January 2014, the valuation of Twitter is
$40 billion IPO.[8] In such a short period of time, have we all got nuts in
valuing companies? Shares hit a high of $73.00 in December 2013. This
was 40 times greater than 2014 projected revenues, or a little more than

1,000 times possible profits. The multiple for 2014 earnings before interest, taxes, deprecation, and amortization (EBITDA) is 285 times. As the tech analysis team at London brokerage, Aviate, told clients at the time of the initial public offering of Twitter: "The opportunity for Twitter is to become the largest real-time delivery system, large enough and pervasive enough to exert noticeable pressure on the overall Internet itself."[9]

Two of the founders, Biz Stone and Evan Williams had their hands in a number of start-ups before launching Twitter. In 1999, Stone helped to launch and grow Xanga.com, a community blogging website. During that same year, Williams cofounded Pyra Labs and launched blogger.com. In 2003, Google acquired blogger.com along with Pyra Labs. Stone and Williams worked at Blogger together at Google until 2004. "I was at Google after selling them Blogger," Williams remembers.

> I stayed there for about 1 year and 8 months. In the first couple months, I hired Biz who had started a somewhat competitive company years earlier. We were working together on Blogger at Google for a couple of years—I left and ended up helping start Odeo.

Odeo Inc. was an online directory for podcasts that also contained tools to help users create and share podcasts.[10] "Basically I followed Ev to Odeo, cause I wanted to keep working with him," Stone said in 2009. "We had started out as rivals but became great friends and really respected each other. So I followed Ev to Odeo."[11]

Prior to joining Twitter, the third founder, Dorsey, worked as a software developer for a number of dispatching companies. In an interview with marketing blog *The Daily Anchor*, Dorsey recalls starting developing such software at age 14. Once Dorsey turned 18, he packed his bags and moved to New York to continue writing dispatch software, now for DMS, one of the largest courier services in the United States. Dorsey was always fascinated by the information that couriers and taxis would send using the dispatch software: it was just the bare essentials, stripped away of peripheral details. Dorsey's early fascination with dispatch software was original inspiration for Twitter's market incubation.

In early 2006, Odeo Inc. was having trouble keeping up with its competitors, a list that included Apple iTunes and other large podcasting leaders. Apple's iTunes would prove to be the major podcasting success, leaving Odeo's future uncertain. "I think we got to a point where it was the right time to start doing new things."[12]

The team at Odeo organized a day-long brainstorming session to conceive of a creative idea that would enable them to reinvent themselves and exit the saturated market they were drowning in. During this session, Dorsey floated an idea to his breakout group: build a service for individuals to send SMS messages to a small network of connections simultaneously. "Dorsey said look I've got this idea," Stone says.

> Look at a buddy list on AIM (AOL Instant Messenger), look at the ten to twelve people you see that are in your list, but just look at their status messages. You get a sense of what everyone's doing even if they're just out getting coffee or sick or too busy to chat or whatever. That's kind of interesting to me. What do you guys think? And it sounded compelling especially when merged with the concept of "what if you could update this status or receive this little status via mobile?"[13]

He imagined it as a city-based service. Using this service, one could, for instance, send a text message to an entire network of friends to advise them on what bar to go to. Odeo was receptive to this idea and Dorsey, Stone, and two other employees were assigned to develop a beta version of the software. Meanwhile, the rest of the Odeo staff would concentrate on their existing products.[14]

On March 21, 2006, Odeo launched the alpha version of Twitter to employees and immediate family. In a blog post called "How Twitter Was Born," former Odeo employee and author of "140 Characters: A Style Guide for the Short Form," Dom Sagolla, recalls how originally there were only about 50 users, but already the service, then called Twitter, felt addictive. "I remember that @Jack's first use case," he writes,

> ...was city-related: telling people that the club he's at is *happening*. "I want to have a dispatch service that connects us on our phones using text." His idea was to make it so simple that you don't even think about what you're doing, you just type something and send

it. Typing something on your phone in those days meant you were probably messing with T9 text input, unless you were sporting a relatively rare smartphone. Even so, everyone in our group got the idea instantly and wanted it.[15]

The beta version was launched soon after, allowing full public access.

In October 2006, Williams bought back Odeo Inc. and all of its assets, including Odeo.com and Twitter, from investors at a little more than the $5 million the company had raised: enough for the angel investors to make their money back and for common shareholders to make a modest gain.[16] He created a new company called Obvious Corp. The team regarded Twitter as a project with high potential; the service would be spun-off as its own company by April 2007.[17]

Twitter's first big breakthrough happened in 2007 at the South by Southwest Interactive Conference and Festival, in Austin, Texas. Twitter strategically placed two 60-inch plasma screens in the conference hallways, streaming twitter messages regarding the conference. Conference goers, speakers, and bloggers tweeted throughout the festival. Reaction to the service was excitedly positive and is often casually cited as the crucial turning point in Twitter's early growth.[18] Twitter employees accepted the Web Award at the conference. Dorsey delivered the acceptance speech, "We'd like to thank you in 140 characters or less. And we just did!" By the end of the festival, Twitter messages went from 20,000 to 60,000 per day.[19]

Twitter received its first round of funding in June 2007 from Union Square Ventures, Charles River Ventures, and a group of angel investors including Marc Andreessen. These funds were used to "grow (Twitter's) resources and focus on the important tasks ahead."[20]

Growth Stage

Twitter began to attract mainstream attention in late 2007 and early 2008. The company received its second round of funding in June 2008, a sum of $22 million, from Amazon founder Jeff Bezos and Spark Capital. The funds were put toward scaling the program for mass adoption.[21]

One of the most interesting impacts of the proliferation of Twitter is the pervasive extent of end-user innovation throughout the service. Many of Twitter's popular social taxonomies and short forms were not invented at Twitter's headquarters, but emerged from the users themselves. For instance, the use of the hashtag symbol (#) as a categorical tool and the @ [name] system as a method of directing tweets to specific users were started by Twitter users. Users continue to employ creative solutions for complex expressions within the boundaries of the simple platform that Twitter provides. This is important beyond curiosity—these innovations have allowed businesses to take full advantage of the network—particularly through sentiment analysis, direct communications with clients and customers, viral marketing, and the identification of strong brand leaders.

Later in the summer of 2008, Twitter realized an expanding popularity for its search functionality. While Twitter began as a service to follow a network of users, it quickly grew into a service for people to follow ideas, concepts, events, and news, particularly through the use of the hashtag system of classification. Following this, the company acquired the leading Twitter search engine, Summize. Summize developed a feature for users to search through a live stream of tweets. The five Summize engineers moved to San Francisco to work closely with the Twitter team and further develop the well-received service.[22]

The other leading social network at the time, Facebook, recognized the potential synergies it could leverage through Twitter and offered to acquire the company for $500 million in stock. However, Twitter turned this down. One of the major drivers of this decision was that Twitter disagreed with Facebook's self-evaluation of $15 billion. It believed that Facebook was worth closer to $5 billion, which would decrease the strength of the deal from $500 million to $150 million. Additionally, Twitter concluded that the timing was not right to sell. They wanted to turn a profit and drive further growth, in order to be offered a larger sum of money sometime in the future.[23]

Twitter was forced to deal with their first communication crisis in July 2009. A hacker gained access to an e-mail account of a Twitter employee and seized over three private company documents, and offered them to bloggers and online publishers. Many media websites followed the story, and TechCrunch actually published a few of the documents. One release forecasted $400,000 profit in Q3 2009, and $4 million profit in Q4 2009. The leaked document also forecasted a user base of 1 billion in

2013.[24] Twitter leadership was contemplating suing the hacker and the news sites that distributed their private data. Michael Arrington, founder and coeditor of TechCrunch, stated that any illegal or unethical activity must be blamed, "on the person who took the information and distributed it. On our end, it was simply news."[25]

Demographics

By summer 2011, a Pew Research Center reported that 13 percent of American Internet users were on Twitter—a figure up 5 percent from the year before that. However, over the course of that year, explosive growth came from Internet users in Indonesia, Brazil, and Venezuela. According to comScore in 2011, the majority of Twitter users are 35 years or older. Twitter user age demographics tend to skew toward Gen-X and older : 26- to 34-year-olds make up 30 percent of Twitter users. The second biggest age group is the 35- to 44-year-olds, comprising 27 percent of Twitter users. 18- to 25-year-olds make up 13 percent of users.[26]

It is also important to note that user-end creativity on Twitter is much more subtle than what is allowed on other, more open sites. For instance, outside of well-written irreverent tweets, perhaps the two most prominent forms of creativity on Twitter come through the use of hashtags and accounts pretending to be written by people they are not, such as historical figures.

Twitter saw tremendous growth from 2007 to 2009. The largest growth year over year was June 2008 to June 2009, users grew from 1 million to 21 million, a 1928 percent increase.[27] After 2009, it continued to grow exponentially and in the summer 2010, figures pegged the number of registered users at 165 million. While Twitter did not release many numbers relating to user numbers in 2011, some industry estimations numbered around 250 million registered users.[28] In September 2011, Twitter announced that there were over 100 million active users. This increase in growth in its early growth acceleration years does come with its disadvantages. There have been countless short outages while the company scales the service to provide for the enlarged user base. When users experience an outage, the famous, "Fail Whale" image (an error message), created by Yiying Lu, pops up on the screen.

Growth continued rapidly for Twitter, with revenues of $1.39 million posted in 2011 to over $405 million posted in 2013. With over 645,750,000 Twitter users as of January 2014, over 135,000 new users onboarding daily, and over 58 million tweets going out daily,[29] Twitter is fast becoming a preferred alternative microblogging channel compared to Facebook.

Tools and Applications

Twitter's API allows for third-party web service and application to integrate with Twitter. Users and companies have collectively created over 100,000 applications, utilizing a simple platform to expand the functions and communication media available.

Developers have created applications and tools to cater to businesses launching social media campaigns. The most popular application to manage one's account is called TweetDeck. The application integrates with Facebook and allows users to sort their tweets by direct message, topic, keyword, and groups. Users can set up a column for mentions of their company and another column for mentions of their competitors. In May 2011, TweetDeck was purchased by Twitter for a rumored $40 to $50 million.

A second application, Bit.ly, enables you to track how many people click on your links. The data provided allows you to decipher which links interest your clients, so you can better plan for tweet topics in the future. A third communication tool is called twitcam. Users post a video of a live broadcast on Twitter and chat with other Twitter users from the broadcast page. A company could request that their customers post questions in regard to a new product and a company representative could respond live through video. There are thousands of applications developed to fit numerous business gaps.

The Democratization of the Media

One of Twitter's most popular and useful functions is the ability to conduct real-time search of tweets. In April 2009, Twitter added a search bar to their interface and a list of trending topics listing the most popular phrases at any given time. Stone explained, "Every public update sent to Twitter from anywhere in the world 24/7 can be instantly indexed and made discoverable via our newly launched real-time search. With this newly launched feature, Twitter has become something unexpectedly important; a discovery engine for finding out what is happening right now."[30] This presents functionality that Google search had not made a serious attempt to tackle until 2011: the ability to search and categorize real-time data streams.

Topics in twitter updates tend to be preceded by a "hashtag" (the # symbol). This is a sort of tacit understanding across Twitter. Plugging in a hashtag will ensure that when a user wants to find, for instance all the tweets about social media, the search #socialmedia, will return up-to-date, user-designated relevant tweets.

External links play a privileged role in Twitter culture. Users expect that a great deal of tweets will be either reposts of other Twitter user's content or will be links to external content. This is one of that factors that has business and marketing professionals looking at influence. It is clear that users build social capital on Twitter, making their mentions and linking much more valuable than those of other users. Measuring this type of influence is difficult and has been approached from a number of different ways. For instance, the company Klout offers analytics to measure the influence of individual user's across their network. Klout develops these analytics by working with a user's network size, the content created, and how people interact with that content (Do they click through it? Do they repost it?). While one user's influence can make some content more valuable than others, the opposite is true as well: because user networks tend to be dynamic, users that publish spam or that do not understand how Twitter operates will likely be unfollowed. This acts as a bottom-up human spam filter.

These three developments have allowed Twitter to democratize media to a great extent. This is particularly true when it comes to news and large-scale events that are of interest to the general public. Twitter now acts as a very fast medium for disseminating news (and often incomplete or misinformation). The most compelling sources regarding important unfolding events tends to rise to the top very quickly.

Between 2008 and 2009, Twitter gained international attention for its widespread use as a news channel. In October 2007, during alarming fires in California, Twitter users would update their followers (who were friends and neighbors) where the fire was minute by minute. In June 2009 when protests were held in Iran in regard to President Mahmoud Ahmadinejad winning the election, the Islamic republic shut down most communication with the outside world. Twitter was used as a powerful tool for protestors to get their stories out.[31] During the election, Twitter was such a vital communication mechanism for activists and cause-advocates that the company was asked by the U.S. administration to postpone a temporary maintenance shutdown.[32] Twitter has become a viable tool in the challenging top-down control from governments that like to control what messages are made public. Similarly, Twitter and Facebook became important tools for protesters in 2010 and 2011 for protesters in Egypt and Syria.

Corporate Accounts and Conferences

Twitter has been a great means to reach out to employees, customers, partners, potential clients, and to keep an eye on competitors. According to an article in *Business Week*, Twitter has dominated chief marketing officers' social network plans.[33] Companies have been increasingly using Twitter to supplement their marketing and communication plans. For some businesses, however, the communication platform is fully integrated into their business model. Kogi Korean BBQ is a taco truck that delivers gourmet tacos to Los Angeles night-goers. The company encountered a problem in 2008; only about 10 people were showing up at each stop, the rest would leave in frustration of traffic hold-ups. The company came up with an innovative solution: the truck driver would send Twitter updates from his cell phone as to when he would arrive at his next specified location. The communication line Kogi developed to keep its customers up-to-date led to 300–800 people lining up per stop.[34]

Contests on Twitter to create awareness have also surged in popularity. Decho, a digital technology company, initiated a contest in the winter of 2009 for its flagship product, Mozy, an online backup service for consumers and businesses. The contest was named "Free Account Friday," whereby users could tweet or retweet a message written by Decho with the hashtag #mozyfaf, at any time on Friday for a chance to win a

Mozy Home account with free backup for a year. Every Monday, Decho announced the winners of the contest and gave a 20 percent coupon to anyone who entered. Since the contest started, @mozy followers have increased from 600 to 3,000 and the company believes that the contest generated between 15 and 20 paid customers per week.[35]

Cross-promotion on Twitter is another marketing solution companies have experimented with. Disney wanted to create buzz around the release of its 70th Anniversary Platinum Edition of its movie Pinocchio on DVD and Blu-ray. The company contacted Melanie Notkin, who runs SavvyAuntie.com, a website community for Professional Aunt, No Kids (PANKS) with more than 8,000 users, which helps readers buy presents for their nieces and nephews. She signed a three-week sponsorship deal with Disney to promote the movie through Twitter updates with trivia contests, giveaways, and posted links to Disney video clips. Disney was very pleased with the results of the promotion and Notkin's followers increased by over 1,000. This is an instance of a giant international corporation partnering with a grassroots organization in an attempt to leverage their ability to disseminate news and advice to a trusting audience. This sort of partnership is becoming increasingly important on the Web.

There are many innovative ideas being experimented using Twitter to increase promotional and brand awareness. Before hashtags were as widespread as they are now, it was unheard of to display a hashtag on the screen for a television program. To promote their "Roast of Donald Trump," Comedy Central displayed the hashtag #trumproast on screen, resulting in 25,000 tweets during initial transmission and driving television viewership higher than it had ever been for that time slot. Other Television shows like ESPN use JavaScript buttons to increase distribution. On each web page, ESPN has a social sharing bar, and then has an additional Tweet button in their media player (nearly every page has a video associated to it). In one month, over 4,000 tweets were generated. Innovative use of JavaScript buttons results in 60,000 additional readers for ESPN every month; this is a very effective way to increase distribution awareness.[36]

These tools are not only being used by businesses, but they are also being used actively by consumers or customers to share their experiences. Not all of them are positive. But the impact on brands is very far-reaching.

Recently, a British Airways passenger named Hasan Syed, frustrated that British Airways lost his luggage and gave him runaround, tweeted "Don't fly @BritishAirways. Their customer service is horrendous." Not content to simply tweet the message, he paid $1000 to promote the tweet resulting in over 73,000 additional impressions and multiple media appearances resulting from the incident. As these social channels continue to increase in popularity, companies need to develop ways to rapidly engage with their consumers and customers to develop approaches that help to restore confidence.[37]

Businesses have frequently used Twitter for market research to conduct virtual focus groups. Another function that Twitter supplies to businesses is the one-to-one conversation a company representative can have with a customer. Direct communication allows a business to reply to and address customer's concerns before they escalate into fires. This also allows for innovative crowdsourcing techniques, whereby companies collaborate with their loyal consumers on product development and other issues. Starbucks was one of the earliest major corporations to turn to Twitter for product innovation ideation.

Many small businesses have used Twitter as their sole means of marketing. It is much easier for a technologically inexperienced small business owner to set up and maintain a Twitter account than a web page. In a 2009 interview with the *New York Times*, writer and web analyst Greg Sterling noted how he saw small businesses using Twitter. "We think of these social media tools as being in the realm of the sophisticated, multiplatform marketers like Coca-Cola and McDonald's," he says. "But a lot of these super-small businesses are gravitating toward them because they are accessible, free and very simple."[38]

Twitter gives entrepreneurs in rural towns the ability to connect with a larger audience. Scott Seamon from Blowing Rock, North Carolina, a partner of Christopher's Wine and Cheese Shop and owner of a bed and breakfast, wanted to broaden his customer base beyond the 1,500 residents in his town. Seamon set up a search on Tweetdeck for people twittering about his town or the mountain nearby. He casually started conversation with these people, and experienced extra traffic to his inn and shop from outside of his town.[39]

Twitter has also evolved into a useful conference tool. The conference "#hackedu" consisted of 40 educators, entrepreneurs, scholars, venture capitalists, and philanthropists discussing the future of education at a conference dedicated to education reform, in Manhattan in 2009. The conference organizers put up a screen during the discussions and invited people outside of the conference who were interested in joining in to send a tweet and include the #hackedu hashtag. The outside tweeters gained an insider perspective on the discussion, as people in the conference would tweet from their laptops and cell phones about what was going on. The outsiders would add comments and questions to the twitter stream, which were then included in the real-time discussion. This process added another layer to the conference. Using Twitter in a conference has three main tangible benefits. First, it documents the conference, secondly, it brought in a larger audience than would otherwise be possible, and thirdly, it gave the conference an afterlife as people continued to tweet about their opinions after the conference ended.[40]

In spring of 2010, Twitter rolled out a new feature and revenue stream, "Promoted Tweets." This marked the beginning of Twitter's advertising platform. Promoted tweets are simply tweets that advertisers have paid to place, and which appear at the top of Twitter search results. "There is one big difference between a Promoted Tweet and a regular Tweet," CEO "Biz" Stone announces to its users in a blog post, "Promoted Tweets must meet a higher bar—they must resonate with users. That means if users don't interact with a Promoted Tweet to allow us to know that the Promoted Tweet is resonating with them, such as replying to it, favoriting it, or Retweeting it, the Promoted Tweet will disappear."[41] They launched the project promoted tweets from high profile companies, such as Starbucks, Best Buy, Virgin America, and Sony Pictures.

In summer of the same year, Twitter rolled out the second phase of its monetization: "Promoted Trends." Twitter has traditionally listed the top-used keywords on the right side of the interface labeled as "trends." Users can change the scale of these top trends, from global to nation to local. The Promoted Trends program allows a company to place a trend at the top of this list. One of the early users of this program was Coca-Cola; their marketing department was impressed. "The amount of impressions in such a short period of time around our whole World Cup campaign," Global Interactive Marketing VP Carole Kruse told the *Financial Times*, "to me it was a phenomenal time." Their Promoted Trend reportedly received 86 million hits within the first 24 hours.[42]

In recent months, Twitter has expanded its advertising program by rolling out a self-service advertising platform for small businesses. At the beginning of April 2012, 10,000 "small business" American Express card carriers were given access to the program, allowing the business owners the opportunity to fund sponsored tweets. American Express partnered with Twitter to launch the new platform, offering their customers early access and $100 credit toward advertising.[43] The system is similar to Pay-Per-Click advertising with Google. On top of this early release, the *Financial Post* noted in April 2012 that Twitter's sales staff "have crisscrossed the country wooing marketing executives at large corporations, from media conglomerates to financial firms and Detroit car makers."[44]

Summary

Twitter executives believe it is important, despite all of the positive media attention they are receiving for the company to stay level headed and humble, and to continue to work on new improvements.

> We don't want to end up like the child actor who found success early and grew up all weird and freaky. We want to remain OK; just because we found success early and in many ways got lucky doesn't mean we're all a bunch of geniuses. It means what it means.[45]

Twitter has used the concept of social networking to develop a simple platform that users mold to their individual needs. The service has aided individuals and businesses alike to connect with a wide audience and has had an important impact on the way that communications have been revolutionized in the 21st century. At this point, their revenue model is maturing, with a valuation approaching $40 billion—Twitter is a force to be admired. What is clear, however, is that Twitter, like Facebook, is changing how people and companies understand value. We're seeing new ways of measuring and tracking user engagement. At the same time, Twitter is contributing to new understanding of grassroots influence and developing an understanding which members of a company's network or user base is most influential. There is no question that microblogging will continue to evolve in interesting and surprising ways. The opportunity to broadcast short communication bursts and connect with anyone anywhere has millions of people engaged in new conversations that were previously never possible.

Discovery Questions

1. Where do you think Twitter will go next in adding new functionality to their platform?
2. What approach have you seen in Twitter usage that you might be able to apply in your organization?
3. What form do you see the next social phenomenon taking?
4. Do you think Twitter and Facebook will merge in the future to keep a competitive edge? If so, why?

CHAPTER 4

LinkedIn

Founded

December 2002 and launched on May 5, 2003.

Founders

Reid Hoffman, Cofounder and Chairman
Allen Blue, Cofounder and VP Product Management
Konstantin Guericke, Cofounder
Eric Ly, Cofounder
Jean-Luc Vaillant, Cofounder

Current Management[1]

Jeff Weiner, Chief Executive Officer
Nick Besbeas, Vice President, Marketing
Mike Gamson, Senior Vice President, Global Solutions
Deep Nishar, Senior Vice President, Products and User Experience
Erika Rottenberg, Vice President, General Counsel and Secretary
Kevin Scott, Senior Vice President, Engineering and Operations
Steve Sordello, Senior Vice President and Chief Financial Officer
Shannon Stubo, Vice President, Corporate Communications
Pat Wadors, Vice President, Global Talent Organization

Overview

Public company traded as NYSE: LNKD
Headquartered in Mountain View, California
Revenue: $1.52 billion (2013)[2]

Net income: $26.77 million (2013)[3]
Market capitalization (December 31, 2013): $25.89 billion[4]
Website: www.linkedin.com
Alexa Global Rank (February 2014): 12[5]
Members (February 2014): 277+ million[6]

Timeline

December 2002—Founded
May 2003—Launched
March 2006—Profitable
August 2010—Acquired mspoke ($0.6 million)
September 2010—Acquired ChoiceVendor ($3.9 million)
January 2011—Initial Public Offering
January 2011—Acquired CardMunch ($1.7 million)
May 2011—Traded its first shares
June 2011—33.9 million unique users
February 2012—Acquired Rapportive ($15 million)
May 2012—Acquired SlideShare ($119 million)
June 2012—Hackers steal 6.4 million users passwords
April 2013—Acquired Pulse ($90 million)
June 2013—259 million users in 200+ countries and territories
July 2013—Announced Sponsored Updates

Early Roots[7]

In very simple terms, LinkedIn is a social networking website for people in professional occupations. Reid Hoffman founded the site in December 2002. Today, LinkedIn is available in 20 languages, and as of June 15, 2013, it had 259 million users in more than 200 countries and territories.[8]

Reid Garret Hoffman was born in Berkeley, California to Deanna Ruth Rutter and William Parker Hoffman on August 5, 1967. He attended high school at the Putney School where he farmed maple syrup, drove oxen, and studied epistemology. Reid graduated from Stanford University in 1990.[9]

It was at Stanford that he formed the idea of changing the world through social networking. He began his career in business and entrepreneurship by joining Apple Computers in 1994, where he worked on eWorld. He later moved to Fujitsu after eWorld was acquired by AOL in 1996. With his restless spirit, Reid moved to PayPal as a member of its board of directors, gaining a reputation as an expert at competing effectively in extremely competitive environments. In 2002, after a long tenure at PayPal and reaching the position of vice president, Reid Hoffman made his move. This is where the LinkedIn history begins.[10]

Operating under the slogan *Relationships Matter*, Hoffman set his sights on starting his own company. In late 2002, Hoffman recruited former colleagues from SocialNet and PayPal to work on his new idea. Six months later, LinkedIn was launched. By the fall of 2003, it showed enough promise to attract investors.[11]

The introduction of address uploads in 2004 caused accelerated growth into 2005, giving Hoffman the leverage to introduce LinkedIn's first business lines. Jobs and subscriptions became integral parts of the site. The company also moved into its fourth office in 3 years. With the launch of Public Profiles in 2006, LinkedIn began to stake its claim as the professional profile of record. That same year, the company achieved profitability while core features, like Recommendations and People You May Know, came online.[12]

With the company on cruise control, Hoffman stepped aside to run product and brought in former colleague Dan Nye to lead the company. Shortly after, in 2007, LinkedIn moved to Stierlin Court and opened the customer service center in Omaha.[13]

Growth Stage

LinkedIn became truly global by 2008. It opened its first international office in London and introduced Spanish and French language versions of the site. By 2009, Reid Hoffman required new leadership for the burgeoning business. He brought in Jeff Weiner as president. The former CEO brought clarity to LinkedIn's mission, values, and strategic planning process.[14]

By the time LinkedIn celebrated its eighth anniversary in 2011, LinkedIn's reputation as one of the best in the professional networking business was well known and the business moved to become a publicly traded company on the New York Stock Exchange.[15] Through product inversion and a redesigned site, LinkedIn began an unprecedented rate of product innovation and transformation by focusing in on three key concepts: Simplify, Grow, and Every day.[16]

The history of LinkedIn exemplifies a company that is customer focused, well managed, and innovative. LinkedIn turned 10 years old in 2013 and it is apparent that Hoffman's original business strategy has paid off. The company now has over 259 million members and is growing at a rate of two members per second. However, it is important to note that a company with success of this magnitude could not survive on business strategy alone. LinkedIn is unique in the fact that it provides a solution to a very common barrier in the business world. It provides a medium by which communication can occur without succumbing to the boundaries of time or space.

Purpose

"We believe that the way the world works is fundamentally changing. Professionals need to make faster and better informed decisions in order to perform in an accelerated business environment."[17] From its inception, LinkedIn has been focused on providing a connection between businesses and professionals. The site itself has come a long way from its humble beginnings, but the goal of the site remains rooted in simplicity. LinkedIn has a very poignant mission statement: "To create economic opportunity for every member of the global workforce."[18]

While that mission statement might sound overly ambitious, the cultural values that LinkedIn has adopted as a company allow its employees to set out on a course that promotes success and strives toward the achievement of that mission. Included in those cultural tenets are five values that help LinkedIn create an atmosphere laden with innovation, creativity, and cutting-edge technology:

- Transformation
- Integrity

- Collaboration
- Humor
- Results

Forbes Magazine identifies LinkedIn's "richest and fastest-growing opportunity" as "turning the company's 161 million member profiles into the 21st-century version of a 'little black book' that no corporate recruiter can live without."[19]

The hype around LinkedIn is substantial and with good reason. It is a unique idea and holds a veritable monopoly in the marketplace. There are a handful of imitation sites, but most of those sites are geared toward a specific group of professionals. For example, the military has a system similar to LinkedIn, which is called "Rally Point." There are also social networking sites that specifically target college basketball recruiting and education providers.[20]

However, none of these sites offers the magnitude of users, both individual and corporate, that LinkedIn does. LinkedIn is a social networking tool that applies to the masses, not just to a specific group. It is also widely accessible; it needs only an Internet connection to function.

Accessibility

LinkedIn is accessible to all cultures and personality types. Every career professional can be connected with LinkedIn, serving as a portal bringing business organizations as well as professionals together in one location. Building a network and being accessible through LinkedIn's website can be accomplished through a simple relationship. LinkedIn is an avenue that one can use to achieve many ends, such as access business connections for buying or selling, connect with potential employees or start a new career, or make a cold call a warm welcome.

Navigating and interacting in and around LinkedIn is quick and easy. LinkedIn ensures all business professionals have access by providing tools for individuals who are blind or have low vision. Image descriptions are used in lieu of text giving them a viable alternative.[21] The applications platform provides additional online aspects that can be embedded in a profile page. These applications consist of Six Apart, WordPress, TypePad, and Amazon.[22]

LinkedIn's social business site provides a variety of pathways to access it. The LinkedIn Mobile App is compatible with iPhones, iPod touch devices, iPads, Android, BlackBerry and Palm devices, and the HP touch-pad. Mobile versions are available in other languages, such as French, English, Chinese, German, Spanish, and Japanese. The newest service for iPhone users allows a person to read e-mail messages through the native iOS Mail Program. Another mobile app called CardMunch features the capability to scan business cards and merges the information into contacts.

Employers should encourage their employees to join LinkedIn; this social business site is a vital tool in engaging a soft marketing technique. LinkedIn provides employees with an avenue to access other professionals for advice, tips, encouragement, mentorships, and more. An organization can take full advantage of enlarging their digital brand across LinkedIn amid employees' profiles. Employees can visit about their role at a company, which can potentially become a valuable lead to a future customer.

LinkedIn paves the way to build prospects by empowering employees to network among a professional social network for business purposes. LinkedIn users are there for a reason, a purpose, or a goal, and that is to engage with like-minded professionals. LinkedIn is a tool where professionals can converse with ease, build a rapport and collaborate in an arena where before they know it, they have connected with a buyer or seller, marketed their organization, mentored another or been a recipient of mentoring, just found the next candidate for an open position, or found themselves a job. The vast functionality of LinkedIn provides an avenue for all to grow professionally, individually, and companywide.[23]

Value to the Individual

LinkedIn offers an individual the ability to build and maintain a wide network of professionals. Much like Facebook, LinkedIn allows members to reconnect with classmates and former colleagues. Those relationships, which are based on your abilities and character, define your reputation. After all, you are building a brand and that brand is you.

A LinkedIn profile allows anyone to see the user's skills, interests, and experiences. A member's account functions like an online resume that is working for the user all the time. Members have a place to showcase groups that they belong to, honors or awards they have received, affiliations or memberships, and professional interests. LinkedIn allows recruiters and HR professionals to examine potential employees that fit their criteria.

A LinkedIn account makes it easy to search for a new career. A member can search for information about different companies. LinkedIn uses detailed company profiles that not only list company statistics, but also recent promotions, hires, and lists of employees connected to the user. The individual can also use the network to identify which skills are the most important for certain industries or positions.

Users can search for job postings on the LinkedIn website. While this is a feature offered by many companies, a huge benefit of being a member of LinkedIn is that many job posts are exclusive and they are not advertised elsewhere. Those postings often have a prerequisite that you have one or more LinkedIn recommendations.[24] There is also a possibility that a LinkedIn member from your network now works there or knows somebody that does, giving you a leg up on the competition for an interview. How does this social network benefit its users? Because of the proliferation of media outlets, more and more companies are looking for word-of-mouth recommendations.[25] Believe me these companies are listening.

Staying connected with old friends and acquaintances is not the only benefit LinkedIn has to offer. If you learn how to use LinkedIn correctly you might find yourself more connected than you could have imagined.

Value to a Business

Most people believe that LinkedIn is the corporate professionals' version of Facebook, and they are correct to a point. While LinkedIn and Facebook share some similarities, businesses are catching on to the huge upside of LinkedIn. What is it about LinkedIn that makes it an effective business tool? Here are several examples:

- LinkedIn allows companies to attract new talent. For a small annual fee, companies can upgrade their membership to add videos and other tools that allow them to inform members about their company, culture, and employees. That helps with recruitment. Companies can also post exclusive job openings. Whether they are actively looking for new talent or not, LinkedIn is the site to find the connections to grow a business.

- Through the use of LinkedIn's company pages, a company can attract potential employees. In addition, this option also gives the company access to individuals who seem like a good fit. LinkedIn offers the company detailed statistics about the company's followers. This allows a company to contact an individual directly to establish that connection.[26]

- Through the use of LinkedIn's company page, you can establish the creditability of your company. LinkedIn allows all of your social media updates to be centralized on the company overview. This allows followers and visitors to learn about what you do and how well you do it. You can also work with users in the answer and group sections. This allows you to show users how your company operates and answer questions from other members or about your industry.

- LinkedIn also provides a dedicated section to expand your marketing footprint. This space allows you to provide information about your products or services and links to your website. LinkedIn also allows you to run custom marketing campaigns based on your industry, title, geographical location, and many other sectors. LinkedIn also allows you to post coupons, discounts, videos, and recommendations from customers.

- Want to keep an eye on your competitor? There is no place better that LinkedIn. By keeping an eye on who they are connecting with, and the recommendations they receive you can learn what they are working on. You can also watch their company page and see who has been hired, fired, promoted, and whether they have any job openings. LinkedIn is a great tool for spotting industry trends. With a simple search, you can find demographic and growth information. How fast a sector is growing compared to others as well as how large it is or the average age of someone in that industry. By watching these trends, you may be alerted to new markets or changing trends.

Summary

Technology and social media have, without question, completely changed the face of personal and professional communication methods around the world. The world is more connected than ever, and both businesses and individuals are utilizing new and innovative technology to increase effectiveness, heighten visibility, and decrease costs. One of the avenues that can be used to achieve such ends is LinkedIn.

LinkedIn has become a household term. Most people have heard of LinkedIn and know that it is a professional networking tool. However, the organization and ideas that drive LinkedIn as a company are often not examined. According to the LinkedIn Press Center, LinkedIn's business solutions are based on three basic principles:

- Hire—engage the world's best passive talent.
- Market—engage most effectively with professionals.
- Sell—engage the world's decision makers.

At a core level, LinkedIn is designed to connect employers and employees virtually and without having to go through traditional processes. Employers traditionally have to post a position, accept resumes, sift through resumes, set up interviews, call references, and then begin the process of hiring a candidate. Potential employees have to search multiple avenues for possible jobs that fit their skill set and requirements, then send resumes to these jobs, wait for a call to invite them to an interview, attend the interview, wait for a call to receive a job offer, analyze the job offer, and respond with either an acceptance of the offer or a refusal.

It is a rather extensive process, and new technology like LinkedIn aims to decrease the tedium of connecting employers and employees. Employees can search and apply to multiple job postings without having to access individual websites or newspapers. Employers can search for potential employees based on skill set, location, and past employment history. They can also view recommendations, endorsements, work history, and educational credentials.

Since time is of great value to both individuals and businesses, anything that can save precious time is definitely an asset. To best utilize the technology that LinkedIn offers, it is important to understand the origins of the site, the purpose that LinkedIn strives toward, and the value that LinkedIn offers to both an individual and to a business.

Communication is an age-old tool that societies across history have used to facilitate growth and innovation. Social media has revolutionized communication, as we know it, and is now pervasive in many societies. Social media permeates our personal lives with Facebook, Twitter, Pinterest, and many other venues. However, the span of social media is not limited to personal or private use. It has something amazing to offer the business world as well.

Social media and virtual collaboration are irreversibly changing the business landscape on both an individual and a corporate platform. One of the ways to capitalize on that change is to utilize tools like LinkedIn. LinkedIn is user-friendly, inexpensive, and widely available. Although LinkedIn is not the cure-all for finding that perfect job or the ideal candidate, it does offer the user a simple and efficient means by which to connect to an entire network of individuals, companies, and groups. The virtual age is upon us, and it is here to stay. LinkedIn has something to offer every user. All the user has to do is to get out there and take advantage of the opportunity.

Discovery Questions

1. What differentiates LinkedIn from other social media platforms?
2. LinkedIn seems to emphasize the need for speed model. Do you agree with their operating principle of "Professionals need to make faster and better informed decisions in order to perform in an accelerated business environment?"
3. How can LinkedIn help business create value?
4. Thinking as a CEO or senior executive, would you encourage your team members to use LinkedIn? Why or why not?

CHAPTER 5

Myspace

Founded

August 2003, as a division of eUniverse.
Relaunched July 2013, as a division of Specific Media.

Founders

Chris DeWolfe
Tom Anderson
Josh Nerman

Current Management

Specific Media LLC

Overview

Private company owned by Specific Media LLC
Headquartered in Beverly Hills, California
Revenue: Unknown
Net income: Unknown
Market capitalization: Not applicable
Website: www.myspace.com
Alexa Global Rank (February 2014): 892[1]
Members: Unknown

Timeline

August 2003—Founded by eUniverse.
January 2004—Surpasses Friendster in user numbers.

April 2004—Myspace Music debuts and is an instant hit.

June 2005—Passes Google in web traffic.

June 2006—Myspace UK is launched.

August 2006—Google and Myspace reach an advertising deal with $900 million.

Early 2007—MyspaceTV introduced (similar to YouTube videos)

April 2007—Myspace News is introduced.

April 2007—Chinese version of Myspace launches.

January 2008—Myspace Russia is introduced.

September 2008—Myspace offers free music downloads to user profiles.

April 2009—Chris DeWolfe steps down as CEO; replaced by Owen Van Natta.

May 2009—Facebook overtakes Myspace in unique visitors per month.

June 2009—Myspace lays off 30 percent of U.S. staff and 66 percent of international staff.

June 2011—Sold to advertising company Specific Media for $35 million.

July 2011—Specific Media enlist Justin Timberlake in planning the future.

August 2011—Ranks 91st most visited site by Alexa, down from 10th in 2009.

June 2013—Myspace relaunches with a new platform UI.

Early Roots

In the decade since Myspace's founding, the site has not only grown and fallen as the Internet's most popular social site, but has also contributed significantly to the revolution of how we work and live. The early roots of Myspace remain somewhat contentious. The company's three founders, Brad Greenspan, Chris DeWolfe, and Tom Anderson, each have different versions of how their startup came to be. The definitive accounts of the story, Angwin's *Stealing Myspace* and Lapinski's *Myspace: The Business of Spam 2.0*, give us salient insights on the company's roots. From these stories, we can extract key lessons of one of the most important sites fueling the evolution of Web 2.0.

In 1999, Tom Anderson and Chris DeWolfe were working at XDrive, a free online storage space. DeWolfe was in charge of XDrive's marketing group, comprised of over 80 employees and Anderson worked as a copywriter. However, the company did not survive the dot com bubble burst and the two were laid off, along with the entire marketing division.[2] Shortly after leaving XDrive in 2001, DeWolfe, Anderson, and XDrive veteran Josh Berman formed an e-mail marketing startup called Response-Base. ResponseBase would be made up initially of former XDrive marketing employees: "Specifically," writes Trent Lapinski, "the employees who had been responsible for the production of XDrive's e-mail newsletter Intelligence X. At its peak at XDrive, eight million people subscribed to Intelligence X."[3] ResponseBase would send out direct marketing e-mails for clients, such as Business.com and LowerMyBills.com. Rapidly, they progressed from direct e-mail marketing into e-commerce, as they moved to sell e-books and eventually manufactured goods.

Despite turning profits early on in marketing and e-commerce, ResponseBase was ill-fated: antispamming software was becoming progressively cheaper and more advanced, and antispamming laws were sweeping the United States.[4] Despite ResponseBase's poor performance, eUniverse, an e-mail marketing company headed by Brad Greenspan, acquired the company in September 2002. "eUniverse had a real talent for identifying things that were gonna be hot on the Internet," recalls author Angwin in an interview with Wired, "and not hot in the way that Silicon Valley stuff is hot, but which viral greeting cards with fart jokes on them were really gonna hit it big. They had a really good eye for that kind of low-brow entertainment online."[5] She argues that eUniverse was quite successful at identifying growing trends and imitating them.

According to journalist Trent Lapinski, the social networking site Friendster inspired DeWolfe, Anderson, and Josh Berman.[6] Their experience in marketing compelled them to develop similar functionality with a vision for a much broader reach; one of their most important assets was a massive network of e-mail addresses that had been steadily growing since the XDrive days. It would be less than a year before they developed a working version of Myspace and released it to the public.

The first members of Myspace were eUniverse employees. In an effort to expand the site, eUniverse held a competition to see which employees could get the most new member signups. eUniverse then used its 5 million e-mail subscribers and popular website to promote Myspace. This helped dramatically and created a surge in popularity for the new site. DeWolfe and Anderson also turned to guerilla marketing and word-of-mouth techniques to generate buzz around their site. The duo would allegedly spend their nights at popular Los Angeles clubs scouting new bands and persuading them to use Myspace to market their music. The logic of this arrangement saw both parties benefiting: musicians had access to a free promotional platform—a rare thing at this point—and Myspace gained a reputation from the social weight that many of these bands would carry.[7]

Shortly after new users began signing up, the site experienced performance issues. High traffic caused the site to experience major scaling problems, and it began to degrade in performance. As Angwin notes in *Stealing Myspace*, a lot of the early work on Myspace was done on the fly, propelled by the philosophy "Get it Out Fast, Fix it Later."[8] One such side effect of this philosophy was an accidental competitive advantage: flexibility. The open-endedness of user profile creativeness addressed a latent demand in young Internet users for creativity and self-expression. A key difference between Myspace and its predecessor, Friendster, was that Myspace had not properly prevented users from inputting web markup language in their profiles. This meant that, where profiles of other social networking sites had defined parameters and looked more or less the same throughout, Myspace was allowing users to treat their profiles as personal web pages. One implication of this was that inexperienced web designers were slowing download times with heavy, perhaps incorrectly written, code and objects like music, video, and large photos. Nevertheless, Myspace decided that customizability was what their users wanted and that they would continue supporting it from their end.

Growth Stage

One of the early technical fixes that differentiated Myspace from its competitors was its rapid load times. As Myspace began attracting more users, Friendster's servers were getting bogged down. Friendster's friend networks operated on a "six degrees of separation" model, wherein users were connected to others only through people they already knew—to contacts that they had approved. In this way, a user would see how their connection of friends in their network operated. However, this was a heavy load on Friendster's servers and slowed load times down to 20 to 30 seconds per page. Friendster's model required that users stay truthful in their profiles: fake identities were not allowed. Myspace was clearly very aware that their users favored creativity not only with regard to their profiles, but with their identities as well. Fake, allusive, and humorous identities abounded on Myspace. Rather than clamp down on such use of their service, the team went in the other direction: they, by default, gave everyone the option of being connected to everyone else. Tom Anderson became everyone's first friend on Myspace. With almost everyone being connected to everyone else through Tom, the Myspace team kept load times fast and catered to developing a creative, high energy, and fun atmosphere that other social networks were lacking.

For a small company growing very quickly and needing frequent fixes, it was important for the Myspace team to stay closely in touch with their growing user base. Tom Anderson, a very personable character, was signed into Myspace working almost all the time. As every new user's first friend, Tom helped foster a relationship between Myspace and its users that felt casual and friendly. Tom's personal blog posts embodied community sentiment and reassured users when Myspace would go down for hours at a time (due to the rapid turnaround for their fixes and program development).

Myspace's rise to the top of the social networking phenomenon occurred in its first five months. Only a month after its launch, Myspace added group profiles, unlimited friends, a new look for the bulletin board, and a mail indicator on the system. In October 2003, they further increased functionality by allowing users to comment on photos, hide their online statuses, block friend requests, and moderate comments. In November, Myspace continued to add richer features to the website by adding classifieds, picture ranking, and a user search engine based upon interests.

During the site's growth phase, they remained in close competition with Friendster. The Myspace team kept a vigilant eye on Friendster's moves and acted with them in mind.[9] A major decision that the company needed to address was their revenue model and decide whether it would be based on a paid membership, or on advertising. Angwin believes that it was Friendster's hiring in March 2004 of new CEO Tim Koogle, whose faith in online advertising was well known, that solidified Myspace's commitment to advertising over a "premium services" model.[10] Although Koogle's time with Friendster would only last 3 months, Myspace's commitment to advertising revenue would have long-term implications; with this came a need to shift Myspace's focus from ever-increasing daily sign-ups to increased page views. Switching to an advertising-based funding model meant changing the company's focus from attracting ever more members to boosting page views. As such, the Myspace team dropped membership requirements, opening up member pages to the public.

By March 2004, Myspace announced that they had surpassed Friendster as the dominant social network and by November of the same year, Myspace finally turned a profit. They had signed their fifth million account and 3.5 million people were visiting the site per month. Advertisers were paying roughly $0.20 per thousand views and the cost of displaying a thousand views averaged at about $0.7 per page. "Even with other costs factored in, Myspace was finally breaking even consistently."[11]

The lure of Myspace for advertisers came from the way that the Myspace profiles are structured. Each user has the option of adding information about himself or herself (age, sex, location, marital status, sexual orientation, ethnicity, education, occupation, salary, or whether or not they smoke or drink), giving advertising companies very salient and valuable information to target. The value of this information goes beyond the placement of simple keyword-targeted advertising: the combination of detailed personal preferences and deep social interaction produces data trails that can be used to create nuanced user-behavior models— something that in theory is much more valuable than advertising revenue. Lapinski remarks that "essentially, Myspace users are filling out marketing profiles that are mined by the company that are then presented as these people's personal Web Pages."[12] This point provides some insight into Myspace's later appeal to media giant News Corp. However, Myspace's signature spontaneity and flexibility lacks the predictability and structure characteristic of more rigid network. This would later be a disadvantage for Myspace, making it more difficult to navigate and less effective than competitor networks for producing deep user-behavior analysis.

After surpassing Friendster, the progressive rollouts of new features helped Myspace to continue attracting more eyeballs and stickiness. They became the dominant force of the social web, until September 2006, when Facebook became publicly accessible. By 2007, the two networking sites held the majority of the market share, divided. In the years following Facebook's rise in popularity, the two social networking sites created something of a cultural divide on the Internet. While Facebook was aimed at and most popular among university students, alumni, or prospective students, Myspace had a user base consisting largely of teenagers, musicians, and Internet subcultures. Because of the freedom allowed to users through HTML embedding, Myspace appealed more to young early adopters, and users inexperienced with web designed but eager to try their hands at it. Indeed, some would argue that Myspace was never able to shed their associations with teenagers. By contrast, Facebook kept their profiles rigidly structured. Even though both Myspace and Facebook continued to flourish for several years, they were continually competing for more users.

Rupert Murdoch and the News Corp

In 2005, News Corp saw value in acquiring Intermix. Myspace was the online playground for a most coveted advertising demographic: technologically literate 16 to 35 year olds. In a $580 million deal that Greenspan publically opposed, News Corp acquired Intermix and thus the social networking giant Myspace.[13] The deal beat rival corporation Viacom, whose interest in Myspace had been peaked. Greenspan had been ousted as CEO in October 2004 and embarked on a long legal battle against Intermix. When News Corp purchased Intermix, Greenspan was one of the most vocal opponents, arguing that $580 million undervalued Myspace, due not only to its popularity, but also its continuing growth. At this point, the Myspace user base had increased from 16.5 million in June 2005 to 30 million in September.

In 2006, Google and Myspace signed a three-year deal worth $900 million. Google would provide Myspace with search facilities and Google's ad company, AdSense, would supply ad-supported clips for targeted content on the site. An important part of this deal was that Myspace meet a number of traffic quotas. Shortly after the sale, revenues jumped from $1 million per month to $50 million per month, and Myspace began opening offices around the world.[14]

Myspace Music

Music became one of the driving factors of Myspace's popularity. Myspace emerged as a network through which the full spectrum of musicians, from little known bands with no budget to established mainstream successes, could market their music and interact with fans. Already in 2006, Myspace became well known for music profiles. Even after the site's popularity as a network of personal profiles declined, its prominent role as a showcase for musicians remained.

Anderson and his team were confident that Myspace Music was doing for music listeners and the music industry what earlier websites like MP3.com had failed to do. Their network was becoming a collection of hubs for all things music-related, centered around the artists. Myspace users could visit an artist's page to listen to songs, find tour dates, leave comments, and get connected to similar bands that they might not have heard of. "Very few people go to a website looking for bands they've never heard of," said Wolfe, "Myspace Music lets people find music online in the same way they find out about music in person: through their friends."[15]

The Myspace team recognized the role that music played in their brand and began early on partnering with major entertainment corporations. In November 2005, they struck a deal with Interscope Records to launch the joint venture Myspace Records. Indeed, a number of mainstream successes, such as Lily Allen and Sean Kingston, built their initial fan bases on Myspace. Given this widespread association of Myspace with music, Myspace has continued to develop and foster "Myspace Music." By 2010, Myspace Music was in competition with music-social networking hybrids, like Last.FM, HypeMachine, and iTunes. To stay relevant and ahead of the curve, Myspace developed user playlist functions similar to the hybrids. One of Myspace's apps allowed users to create their own playlists, and another acted as an aggregating program to display to users the most popular music in different genres and locations.

Sale to Specific Media, Looking Forward

At the end of June 2011, News Corp agreed to sell Myspace to Specific Media for just $35 million dollars and a 5 percent stake in Specific Media. News Corp selling Myspace for less than it paid for it in 2005 did not come as too much of a surprise to many. Shortly after the acquisition, Myspace began losing money and traffic. In the face of rising competition and accelerated growth, Myspace was forced to cut 400 jobs in June 2009. This job cut occurred during the same week that Facebook surpassed Myspace in number of users. In 2009, Myspace announced that it failed to meet its advertising targets. A year later, News Corp's chief operating officer called Myspace's losses "neither acceptable or sustainable."[16]

In the 2011 *Financial Times* article, "Murdoch's Myspace Dream Turns to Dust," Matthew Garrahan attributes the site's downfall to "years of management mis-steps, the rise of Facebook and clashes between the News Corp hierarchy and Myspace managers."[17] In a 2009 piece, Garrahan sets Myspace's close, casual relationship with its user-base against News Corp's financial goals and competitiveness,

> [Myspace] prided itself on being able to respond quickly to the needs and demands of its community, but once Murdoch had set the $1bn revenue target, putting the Myspace community first became more difficult. According to former Myspace executives, the advertising on the site was making it less compelling for users. Meanwhile, any innovations or changes that might have cut the number of page views—and therefore advertising revenues—were likely to fall foul of News Corp.[18]

Former Myspace CEO Mike Jones, looked back in 2011 and told CNN Money that, tensions between Myspace and News Corp considered, a major rebranding would have prevented the site's downfall. "We found that regardless of how much we improved the product or the marketing message," he said, "consumers' memories about the brand were too strong to allow them to view Myspace with fresh eyes and an open mind. . . .We could not escape their images of animated GIFs."[19]

After News Corp sold Myspace in 2011, Specific Media announced that pop star Justin Timberlake would have ownership stake in the company. "We look forward to partnering with someone as talented as Justin Timberlake," Specific Media CEO Tim Vanderhook said in a statement, "who will lead the business strategy with his creative ideas and vision for transforming Myspace."[20] The company made it clear that they would be focusing on entertainment in their revamping of Myspace.

The new platform launched on June 2013. The look and feel of the environment and how it organized information and imagery was drastically different from the original platform. The new Myspace is clean with a platform-wide aesthetic vision and a clear focus on digestible content. In contrast to the hodgepodge of personal sites that characterized the old Myspace, users experience the new platform as thumbnail style squares and rectangles laid out on a horizontal grid. Users can browse through the image-blocks representing people or bands. This is a layout that would be familiar to tablet users—as it is currently a popular way of laying out magazines on tablets. It is also reminiscent of how iTunes displays albums in their online store. The main navigation is a simple set of persistent links on the left-hand side of the screen—allowing users to browse "Featured Content," "People," "Music," "Mixes," "Videos," and "Radio." At the bottom of the screen is a persistent media player. In terms of user experience, it is clear that the revamp is about delivering content in a professional and compelling way.

At the end of 2013, Myspace's "Facts and figures" sheet online comprises only of musical data, showcasing that they are home to 14 million unsigned artists. At this time, however, it is important to mention that Myspace is no longer the de facto online presents for musical artists. Many musicians have chosen services like Bandcamp, which are very minimal esthetically and focus primarily on allowing people to sample music and buy digital files quickly.

Summary

Myspace came early to be known for its "laid-back and anti-authority" vibe.[21] This carefully managed relationship with its user-base allowed Myspace to explode in popularity beyond its predecessor and competitor,

Friendster. By interacting closely with their users and taking their suggestions and complaints into account in real time, Myspace satisfied a widespread but latent growing demand for online social creativity and new forms of community. However, this may have also contributed to Myspace's eventual downfall once bought out by media giant News Corp. It is clear that Myspace's "get it out quick, fix it later" philosophy that went hand in hand with its "laid-back" feel could not continue to coexist with the aggressive advertising targets set out by the Myspace–Google deal or with News Corp's own targets. Indeed, neatness and professionalism were early qualities that attracted users to Facebook. Despite widening demographics and increasing popularity, Myspace has always had difficulty shaking public associations of the company with adolescence and rebellion.

Although Myspace was handed its fair share of troubles, the company has been undeniably influential. The Internet has trudged on from the dot com bubble burst, and Myspace is an example of something that came out of that and changed the way people live their lives online, and how social networking sites are turning a profit. Their early innovation insights helped develop a more attractive market opportunity for Facebook and many other social networking sites. As we know in innovation, the long-term winners are seldom the early market giants.

Discovery Questions

1. Based on what you have read, what other business factors in play impacted Myspace's sustained growth? What could they have done differently to ensure their market leadership was stronger?
2. What other lessons can be learned given the meteoric rise and decline of Myspace?
3. What interventions could the board of directors have created to mitigate the value erosion of Myspace?
4. Do you think Myspace will be able to successfully transform itself? If so, why do you think so?
5. Is it possible for a giant platform to transform itself when it is already home to massive amounts of social data? At what point does that become too heavy to be able to pivot?

CHAPTER 6

WordPress

Founded

Initial release May 27, 2003.

Founders

Matt Mullenweg
Mike Little

Current Management

Ryan Boren, Bug Whisperer
Mark Jaquith, Director of Whitespace
Matt Mullenweg, Head of Bug Creation
Andrew Nacin, Entomologist in Residence
Andrew Ozz, Tiny Manly Code Editor (MCE)
Peter Westwood, Title Rebuilding

Overview

Open Source project
Headquartered in the Web
Revenue: Unknown
Net income: Unknown
Market capitalization: Not applicable
Website: www.wordpress.com and www.wordpress.org
Alexa Global Rank: 19[1] & 73[2]
Members (December 31, 2013): Not applicable

Timeline

January 2003—Mullenweg announces plans for b2 redevelopment.

May 2003—Mullenweg and Little release WordPress.

August 2005—Mullenweg founds Automattic.

November 2005—Automattic launches WordPress.com.

April 2006—Automattic raises $1.1 million in funding.

November 2007—WordPress wins award for "Best Social Networking."

September 2008—Automattic acquires IntenseDebate.

November 2008—Automattic acquires Polldaddy.

February 2011—WordPress 3.0 is downloaded 32.5 million times.

March 2011—WordPress blogs receive 520 million visitors per month.

July 2013—Mullenweg reports WordPress powers an estimated 18 percent of the Web.

July 2013—WordPress is downloaded 46 million times per year.

Early Roots

In the early Web 2.0 days, WordPress emerged with a value proposition that contrasted its predecessors and competitors. While rival Blogger had developed a service that was extremely user-friendly, WordPress appealed to a market looking for a sophisticated and customizable user interface. At that time other services like Movable Type were flourishing. However, WordPress soon dominated the market as an open-source blogging solution that offered ownership and security. According to WordPress, the service was born out of a "desire for an elegant, well-architecture personal publishing system."[3] The start-up delivered dynamic service by conducting the project on an open source platform. Internet users worldwide have access to the software's source codes and as such WordPress.org exists as a community of users and developers. Thousands of developers have contributed to the software's design, development, themes, and plug-ins.

WordPress.org grew out of B2/Cafelog, a blogging platform created in 2001 by Michel Valdrighi. In June 2002, Matt Mullenweg, a high school saxophone player, used the B2/Cafelog software to document a trip to Washington, DC. While experimenting with the software, he contributed some minor code to help clean it up. He continued to use the software until going away to university. Soon Mullenweg began his first year at the University of Houston.[4] "I was a terrible student, which means I was spending most of my time on the computer . . . and one of these things was blogging," Mullenweg recalls in an interview with Revision3. "It was Michel that ran the [B2/Cafelog] project," WordPress cofounder Mike Little says in a 2010 discussion on WordPress's history, "pretty much he was the only direct developer. His real life intruded and he literally disappeared off the map. Even people who knew him personally didn't know where he was. It was at least two months before anyone heard from him. Personally people were concerned about what was going on with him, because you got to know his personality, like you do with people online sometimes.[5] "The domain was coming up for expiration," Mullenweg adds, "so we were not even sure if the website was going to be around." During this period of uncertainty, Mullenweg announced on his blog that because B2/Cafelog had ceased to develop their software, he was going to begin working on it as an open source project. He planned to bring it up to web standards and apply some of his own ideas. Mike Little, a UK developer and B2 forum user, contacted Mullenweg, and the two formed WordPress.org with B2/Cafelog as their base. "The good news is," Mullenweg says, "that [Michel] was fine. He came back and saw WordPress and said 'this is really cool. This is the official continuation.' "[6]

Looking back, Little says they felt like they had just gotten started. The first release had not yet even dropped and the pair had become the official successors to the software.

Growth Stage

One of the factors in WordPress's initial burst in popularity was good time. Movable Type was introducing a new version of their software: "it was a developer release," Mullenweg says, "so it didn't add any new features, but it did sometimes increase the cost significantly for people. We were lucky to release our 1.0 version—with a MoveableType importer— about a week later. Very fortunate timing."[7]

A crucial point in WordPress's monetization came in 2005, when Mullenweg founded a new company called Automattic. This would be a key WordPress contributor and also be a way to commercialize the software.

"What would happen," he asked, "if we could make a version of Word-Press [for which] you didn't need to know frp, htp, or MySQL to use?"[8] In the beginning, WordPress was aware that their software was hitting a limited developer market. WordPress.org users need to be able to upload the WordPress software to their server, set up a database, and run a configuration script: a process with a considerable learning curve to those unfamiliar with web development. Automattic launched WordPress.com in 2005 as a solution. It was to be a hosted version of WordPress.org that offered a user-friendly experience in competition with Blogger and Movable Type. WordPress.com offers easy set-up without the need to install WordPress software on one's own server. Bloggers using this service do not need to worry about upgrades, backup, antispam measures, and security. However, WordPress.com does not allow the use of custom themes, and users must choose from a list of provided themes—a factor that might sway the average web user.

For Mullenweg, the next major milestones came with their release of plug-in and theme architectures. He is adamant that every mature open source project evolves to include plug-ins. "You can't build everything and there are no more killer features."[9] Currently, the average WordPress blog has five or six plug-ins—suggesting the average WordPress user has an experience tailored to his or her needs. The community of WordPress users develops most plug-ins. Shedding away control over the feature possibilities has allowed WordPress to stay at the forefront of what is imaginable in blogging.

Although developed largely by its community members, Automattic has supported the site since 2005. Automattic has also been the company through which Mullenweg has made a number of acquisitions. Their first acquisition was Buddy Press in 2008: an open-source social networking software that can be added to WordPress as a plug-in. This allows users to network with other bloggers through things like group creation, user profiles, and activity streams. Their second acquisition, also in 2008, was IntenseDebate, a blog comment hosting service. The final acquisition that year was Polldaddy: polling technology for users to include on their blogs.

In 2008, Automattic obtained a second round of funding. This time, in the area of $30 million, from a group that included the *New York Times*. On his blog, Mullenweg wrote, "Automattic is now positioned to execute on our vision of a better Web not just in blogging, but expanding our investment in anti-spam, wikis, forums, and more—small, open source pieces, loosely joined with the same approach and philosophy that has brought us this far." Indeed, this allowed the company to set their sites on more small acquisitions and commit to "more aggressive scaling."[10] By September 2011, the company had around a dozen small projects, such as the antispamming software Akismet and the RSS aggregator blogs.

The WordPress Foundation

In 2010, Automattic transferred the WordPress trademark (as well as bbPress and BuddyPress) to the WordPress Foundation: a charitable organization headed by Mullenweg whose mission is to "further the mission of the WordPress open source project: to democratize publishing through Open Source, GPL software."[11] The foundation is also responsible for protecting WordPress WordCamps. This is the unofficial name for WordPress-related gatherings (of all types) that have been organized since 2006. Some of these are formal conferences, while others are informal unconferences. In the past few years, both the number and geographical locations of these conferences have widened greatly. As of the end of 2013, a total of 314 WordCamps had taken place, with 72 happening in the last year.

Security Issues

Being an open source community with independently developed plugins, WordPress has faced a number of security issues. In a major 2008 hack, hackers took advantage of the fact that WordPress is an open source platform and pushed security vulnerabilities. "One such attack actually happened to me back in January 2008," Techcrunch's Cubrilovic writes, "when I noticed that a blog I was hosting had been littered with tens of thousands of pages relating to pharmaceuticals and adult material. Someone had gotten access to the blog and literally created new pages." Developers and users often find vulnerabilities in the code and fix the problem. Traditionally, WordPress has been quick to send urgent upgrade message to its users. However, hackers have, as in Cubrilovic's case, gained access to accounts before users are warned of the problem.[12] Since 2008,

WordPress has often restated their ambition toward more in proactive security measures they take, and is encouraging users to frequently update their blogs to new versions.

Release Three

In 2010, WordPress released Version 3.0. Over the course of the next year, the team accelerated its mobile application reach. By 2011, WordPress was available across six platforms and eight device profiles. At the 2011 "State of the Word" address, Mullenweg reflected on this development: "doing all these mobile apps—and every single one is open source," he said, has allowed them to experiment with the interface in ways they would not have otherwise imagined, because they were able to build them from scratch. For example, the approach they took with WordPress their first mobile application iOs was different from their approach to the most recent, the Windows Phone Seven. On top of expanding horizontally across platforms, the blogging software is being used around the world. "In the United States, one in three people online visit a wordpress.com every month."[13] By September 2011, WordPress 3.2 had been downloaded over 7.7 million times.

On the level of plug-ins, and ease of use, WordPress has a number of advantages over competitors like Blogger. In WordPress's 2011 "State of the Word" address, Mullenweg announced some results from a global survey. Regarding what users liked best about WordPress in general, the answer "ease of use" dominated the results. However, it is WordPress's commitment to open source that has allowed them to rise far above their competitors. This is so not only in the way of plug-ins, themes, and intelligence design, but also in the community spirit that manifests throughout. Reading Mullenweg's blog posts and listening to his interviews, it is clear that this is something that the Automattic and WordPress Foundation team strive to nurture. Indeed, Mullenweg notes that having a community of developers allowed them to initially push past Moveable Type when the latter company had 150 to 200 employees and WordPress had only 20. "Open Source is the lever," he says. "We have five core contributors to WordPress, but there are 150 people who regularly contribute to the software and thousands who build plugins and add-ons and themes.

There is really quite a large ecosystem. We're able to have a successful platform that's built by probably more developers than Six Apart."[14]

In 2012, WordPress announced a new REST API, giving increased access to information and data to developers. In the two years that followed, WordPress would continue enhancing developer capabilities. In his 2013 "State of the Word Speech," Mullenweg announced that WordPress 3.7 would be released as an application platform.[15] This has allowed developers to extend the capabilities of WordPress to accommodate functions like e-commerce, learning management, and customer relationship management. The present reality of WordPress is that it is being used for much more than blogging and content management, giving the brand a more multifaceted and complex identity than a few years ago.

For users jumping into WordPress in 2014, they are entering a universe of plug-ins, themes, professional development and design services, and global community. First-time users must learn the WordPress software—or hire someone to do so—and also discern which among the thousands of plug-ins are of the best quality and are most appropriate for their needs. Are they going to be using WordPress as a blog, e-commerce, or portfolio? Is it the best system for their needs? What are their alternatives?

In 2013, WordPress was downloaded 46 million times. Sixty-nine percent of people who were using it treated it as a fully fledged content management system, as opposed to simply a blogging platform.[16]

"I would like a large percentage—over a majority—of websites in the world to go through WordPress," Mullenweg said in 2011. This is an important goal to keep in mind when reflecting on the lessons learned from WordPress. They have become one of the major players in online blogging through slow and careful growth, a commitment to open source and collaboration and through innovative revenue models. "If you build things in such a way that you enjoy the journey as much as the end goal, even if you end up in a different place than you expected—as most businesses do—you loved every day of it and you are proud of everything you did along the way," Mullenweg tells Jason Callacanis, "Even if Automattic were to go out of business—gets hit by a meteor or something—WordPress the software would still be out there and free and would continue to add value to business and to personal lives."[17]

Discovery Questions

1. Do you agree with WordPress's contention that there are no more killer applications? What does this mean for how companies treat blogging? Should policy address the use of user-generated applications versus those developed by established companies?
2. What lessons can you take away from the way that WordPress has structured itself as a brand as well as a collection of different entities?

CHAPTER 7

Blogger

Founded

Launched August 23, 1999 at Pyra Labs.

Founders

Evan Williams
Meg Hourihan

Current Management

Google

Overview

Pyra Labs is a subsidiary of Google
Headquartered in San Francisco, California
Revenue: Unknown
Net income: Unknown
Market capitalization: Not applicable
Website: www.blogger.com
Alexa Global Rank (February 7, 2014): 53
Members (December 31, 2013): Unknown

Timeline

August 1999—Pyra labs launches Blogger.
February 2003—Google purchases Blogger for an undisclosed amount.
May 2004—Signed for a product integration with Picasa Hello.

August 2006—Google launched their newest version of Blogger in beta.

December 2006—The new version of Blogger is taken out of beta.

May 2007—The service was completely moved over to Google servers.

May 2009—Blogger allows BlogSpot users without their own registered domain to sign up with AdSense.

July 2011—Google tracks monthly unique visitors at 4.9 billion.

December 2013—7.3 percent of websites in the Alexa Top 1M use Blogger.

Early Roots

In the middle of the dot-com boom, Meg Hourihan and (later Twitter cofounder) Evan Williams built Pyra Labs. Originally, Pyra Labs was interested in creating a project management, contact management, and to-do list software called *Pyra*. While building Pyra the team used a simple in-house note-taking program that would soon take center stage and be known as Blogger: one of the first applications for creating and managing blogs.[1] "Blogger," says cofounder Evan Williams, "was a side project. It was a very simple idea: you could type something and hit a button and it posts on the Web. We didn't invent weblogs, but we thought 'that's a neat idea, lets write this little application to make it easy to do that, and maybe if people see that, they'll find out about our real product.' "[2]

"Everyone was getting funded [in 1998]," Williams told author Jessica Livingston in 2008, "but it is still completely just a network. You have to know the right people . . . we were just from a different place and not hooked up into that at all. So we just said, 'OK here is the product we are going to build,' and we started building it."[3] Williams explains that he had personal contracts with companies like HP and Intel that he turned into Pyra contracts to keep the company going. The first year was self-funded. "HP basically funded Pyra for the first year unbeknownst to them," he says.[4]

At the start of 1999, Meg Hourihan began working with Williams full time and in May they rented an office and hired their first employee.[5] Around 1999 and 2000, people were indeed blogging. But it was a medium" that lacked accessibility for would-be blog writers. There was no simple platform for publishing, and as such, bloggers needed to be web savvy enough to input all of the required HTML coding. "GeoCities made is easy to have a website," Williams recalls, "but they didn't make it easy to publish anything on an ongoing basis."[6] Williams wrote up a script to tweak that process and used it for his own site. Having the means to easily and immediately publish a thought was a game changer. Automating that process completely changed the experience of operating a website.[7]

Williams and Hourihan began using the script for their own internal publishing—a blog called *Stuff.* "It was a place where we collected things," Williams remembers, "and as we grew, it was the center of Pyra. It was where things happened."[8] While Pyra developed their complex collaboration software for clients, the team continued to derive a lot of us out of their internal blog Stuff. Soon after, Pyra's first employee, Paul Bausch added a new functionality to Stuff: the ability to publish select content externally. "We were one of the first companies to have a blog on our site—not that many people were reading. But it was neat."[9] In 1999, they decided to turn their tool into a product. However, focusing on developing the application took some time, as it seemed too simple, too trivial.[10] In his interview with Livingston, Williams recalls regretfully how he and Bausch built and launched Blogger in one week—the week that Hourihan was on vacation. Her August 24, 1999 blog post is titled, "A new tool for publishing websites," and consists simply of a link to Blogger with a note in parentheses, "I didn't help build it."

Blogger was made available initially as a free service with no revenue-generating model, and it caught on quickly. But for the Pyra team, this posed a problem because their actual product was still struggling. Williams explained that their goal with Blogger was not to simply "attract eyeballs," as was a driving motivation during the dot-com boom.[11] To pursue that kind of business, they would have had to raise money, which they never did. "So we very clearly had a dilemma on our hands: we could focus on the stupid little Blogger app that people were using or we could work on our real product. We tried to split our time amongst those two things and contracted to pay the bills."[12]

Once the staff at Pyra Labs had gone through all of their financial resources, they were left with no choice but to work without pay. But it was clear that Blogger was an important tool. "It just sort of exploded from there," recalls Hourihan, "I guess culturally the timing was right . . . [The Web] was becoming part of everybody's consciousness or awareness, and so then when they decided, 'Hey, I want to be part of this web, how do I participate in it?' blogs were seen as the way to do it."[13] The original Blogger interface was very simple. "A box and a button," says Hourihan, "It was very small; it looked almost exactly like what Twitter is now."[14]

During this time, Pyra was not making any money off of Blogger. In 2000, however, they were able to raise some money. Williams explains that they first managed to secure some funds from O'Reilly, for whom Williams had worked for seven months. The team was not yet focusing solely on Blogger, so the funding came to the relief of both the Pyra product and Blogger.[15] In the months that followed, they were able to raise some more significant funds. "We were still able to get money without a lot to go on. We raised a half a million dollars from O'Reilly, Advance. net, Jerry [Michaelski], Meg's parents, John Borthwick from AOL and Jerry's father-in-law. Half a million dollars was a lot of money to us at the time."[16] Hourihan and Paul were "pretty much pro-Blogger" at this point, though Williams remained on the fence, not entirely sure if he wanted to give up on the Pyra product he had worked so much on.

The other factor that made a pure Blogger focus difficult was that it was not based on any new technology. Compared to Pyra, Blogger was a very simple, almost trivial tool. For Williams, the turning point came when he realized that even though blogging was not new tech, it was somehow tuned into something primal about the Web—something that the Web was naturally good for. "It was about freshness and frequency, and it was about the democratization of media and giving power to everybody and the universal desire for personal expression and the attraction to a real compelling personal voice."[17]

With funding and a new commitment to Blogger, the team grew to seven people and focused building the product and developing a community around it. Although the dot-com crash was real and happening around them, it did not really discourage the team. "The extent of the crash didn't dawn on us that quickly," Williams says.[18] Rather, they used the $500,000 at their disposal to build momentum. They began following the "attract buzz, make money later" path. As was the case with many websites at the time, they began to run out of money and more funding became very elusive. "We felt connect at the time, but it wasn't necessarily to the money crowd, and we probably wouldn't have been able to talk the talk of VCs anyway. So the money wasn't coming."[19]

As Blogger's funds began to run out, they had to discuss next steps. Williams explains that during the crash, many consumer services began turning to enterprises as clients. An idea that spread quickly through Silicon Valley was that consumers could not support start-ups in such times and the only reliable source of money would be in large companies. Blogger made a deal with Cisco and installed a version of blogger within the enterprise, but Williams explains that the team was not entirely sold on the idea of becoming an enterprise service. They were plugged in, but into a new community of networked citizens—Meg, Evan, and Paul were deep into the idea that their product was changing the world and democratizing media. As such, they did not feel comfortable leaving their consumer service to wither while they focused on enterprise clients. And though they had built a version of Blogger with pro features, they did not feel it was good enough to charge money for.

What began as a couple weeks without compensation turned into months—it was clear that Pyra was in trying times. By December 2001, two potential acquisitions had failed and the company was out of money. On January 16, 2001, everyone at Pyra was officially laid off. Nevertheless, they continued to come into work because of their faith in what they had created.[20] "Obviously when you are in that state, tensions rise a lot and morale wasn't good and relationships with my cofounder weren't good," William recalls, "I said, 'I am going to stick around because I took a half of a million dollars of other people's money. And we have all of these users.' "[21] Indeed, the service was still running and growing considerably. In terms of users Google was more successful than ever.

"After I sat with each person and asked them to sign away their rights to all back pay and vacation pay," writes Hourihan on her blog, "and after I explained COBRA and unemployment benefits, and after I thanked them for all their hard work through all the uncertain times, I went into the office bathroom and I burst into tears. And when I got home, I got into my bed and cried and cried and cried."[22] Eventually, the former employees began to seek new employment.

Over the next month, Blogger pursued a very early version of crowd-funding, by asking for donations to help the service run better. They explained on the site that Blogger was running slowly because they were continually getting new users but were out of money to pay for new hardware. According to Williams, the effort was surprisingly effective. Out of several thousand users, 100 or so people gave money, typically larger than the $10 or $20 the team asked for. The publishing company CMP offered to buy them a server worth $4000. "Between the users and [CMP]," Williams says, "we had about $17,00 to spend on servers, which is more than we ever spent of servers, so it was a bonanza."[23]

True to their promises, the money was put only to hardware. Which meant that the team was still unemployed. Tensions were high. By the first of February, even Hourihan left. Her blog posts from the time show that it was anything but an easy decision. "There are only so many days to slog the same path, battle the same unwinnable arguments, endure the same pains and heartaches," she writes. "And then the days run out, either because you die, or you decide enough is enough. Because you decide this is no way to live. Not when this thing called work first devours your life, and then, unstated still, you watch it begin to munch on the lives of those around you, those people that you love very very much. On Monday I resigned from the company I co-founded."[24]

The team had built something that was actively changing the way people communicated on the Internet, but they had no choice but to watch their company disintegrate. Williams was faced with running the company alone, until he secured additional funding. The next day, he came into the office alone and published a short essay called, "And Then There Was One." In the essay he explains that the team broke apart after finally learning that the one acquisition that they were hoping for was not going to happen. "This took the wind out of the already limp sails people were surviving on, and it was largely decided we couldn't keep this up."[25] He assured readers that despite his team moving on, neither Pyra nor Blogger was dead.

> I can tell you, at this point, I definitely plan to keep Blogger going. If you're a Blogger user, you know that things have not been working great with the product for quite a while. I'm not going to

make excuses about that. But I'm not walking away. The good thing is, I have relatively low costs, adequate server power for a while (thank you) and the ability to focus on what I'm good at: Creating things.[26]

Indeed, without having to pay staff, Williams' overhead was quite low and he still had enough money from donations to keep things steady. "I don't pretend I can do all this by myself," he writes, "Nor that this path is going to make my life easier anytime soon. But I can't give up."[27] He finishes his essay asking if anyone in the area would like to lend him some office space.

Williams' blog, EvHead was well read and his essay "And Then There Was One" had a broad audience. Over the next week, he received a flood of e-mail responses with well wishes and offers to help. Funding would eventually come in April 2001 from Trellix, a provider of website publishing technology and hosting services. Following the new inflow of funds, Williams developed ad supported Blogger and Blogger Pro to monetize his services and mitigate the risk of falling into the same difficult situation.[28]

Growth Stage

In early 2003, Williams sold Blogger to Google for an undisclosed amount. Prior to making this decision, Williams was faced with two options: acquire more funding or sell to Google.[29] Williams, following his instincts, chose the latter option. He explains in his blog, the decision allowed much needed "access to these amazing resources (not just money, and servers, and bandwidth, and traffic, and the index, but incredible brains)" and was "dream scenario."[30] Williams continued to work on Google's Blogger as program manager.

After a year of working with Google, Williams felt restless and decided to leave to pursue other career opportunities. Perhaps, as noted in one of his blog posts, it was his "fiercely independent nature." Or perhaps, he was uncomfortable working at an office with a boss and six hundred people when he was used to working for himself with six people.[31] He left to found another company called Odeo Inc., which would later spawn Twitter. Twitter's current rate of growth exceeds that of Facebook adoption.

Summary

In 2014, Blogger is tightly integrated with Google's other products. Any Gmail user can quickly navigate to Blogger among Google's other apps and set up a blog. It is still active and retains the same brand of ease of use and low learning curve. Where Blogger differs from its largest competitor, Wordpress, is in the way that remains a product itself rather than a developer platform. Google is integrating blogger into its other services, whereas WordPress is continually integrating applications from its community of developers.

Blogger is often the blogging platform of choice for first-time bloggers. This is partly a factor of branding and image—it has always carried with it ease of use as a defining feature. However, Blogger has a lot of flexibility in creating and modifying templates and scripts, and so is also suitable for experienced bloggers and web designers.

Discovery Questions

1. Does your organization use internal and external blogging practices? What is working effectively, or not?
2. Do you have full-time internal and external social media experts blogging as professionals in your organization?
3. Do you have an effective social media policy that addresses blogging or microblogging?

CHAPTER 8

YouTube

Founded

February 14, 2005.

Founders

Steve Chen
Chad Hurley
Jawed Karim

Current Management

Salar Kamangar, Google Senior Vice President, YouTube, and Video

Overview

Subsidiary of Google
Headquartered in San Bruno, California
Revenue: Unknown
Net income: Unknown
Market capitalization: Not applicable
Website: www.youtube.com
Alexa Global Rank (February 7, 2014): 3[1]
Members (December 31, 2013): 1 billion unique users visit YouTube
each month[2]

Timeline

February 2005—YouTube.com is registered.
October 2005—YouTube incorporates.

November 2005—Sequoia Capital invests $3.5 million in YouTube Inc.

December 2005—YouTube launches officially.

March 2006—Serving over 200 terabytes per day.

April 2006—Sequoia invests an additional $8 million in YouTube.

September 2006—YouTube hires CFO.

October 2006—Google acquires YouTube for $1.65 billion.

December 2007—YouTube Launches Partner Program.

March 2008—YouTube announces new and expanded APIs.

November 2008—Agreement with MGM, Lions Gate Entertainment and CBS.

June 2009—YouTube launches a movie trailers page.

October 2009—YouTube announces 1 billion views per day.

November 2009—YouTube launches 1080p full-HD video mode.

October 2010—Hurley steps down as CEO, is replaced by Salar Kamangar.

November 2010—YouTube exceeds 2 billion views per day.

November 2011—Google + integrates directly with YouTube.

January 2012—Number of views per day reaches 4 billion.

December 2013—YouTube revenues for 2013 to be $5.6 billion, up 51 percent from 2012.

Early Roots

Acquired by Google in 2006 for $1.65 billion in stock, YouTube Inc. has revolutionized the way that the Internet is being used to view and share online video content. Today, it is ranked the third most visited site on the Internet and users watch upward of 4 billion videos a day.

The roots of the company trace back to 2004, when three employees at PayPal, Chad Hurley, Steve Chen, and Jawed Karim, found themselves in a garage in California, discussing the almost nonexistent state of online digital video sharing. After careful deliberation, the team decided that if there was no easy way to share the dinner party footage they had taken the night before, then they would have to create one. The result would be the fastest growing website in Internet history.

In contemporary Internet terms, the pre-YouTube context is ancient history. The site's founding came about at a time when the capabilities of the Web were changing rapidly. Before 2005, something like You-Tube did not exist because bandwidth and infrastructure limitations would have made it near impossible to maintain and popularize. Karim explained at a conference at the University of Illinois the problems that video sharing faced before they created YouTube. In the first years of the 21st century, broadband was not something that was easily available in the home. He reminds his audience, "a video website, of course, could not work on dial-up." As well, advertising revenue could not easily offset the bandwidth costs of hosting a site like it. That having been said, the pre-YouTube video-downloading environment was such that searching for video files had to be done on search engines like Google, and through that, one could only hope to come across a personal FTP index. Peer-to-peer file-sharing software, such as Bitorrent, was also an option. In both peer-to-peer file sharing and FTP indexes, however, easy user interfaces were sparse, if existent at all.[3]

Sharing personal video content likewise had to be done via a personal website, as the files would have been too large for e-mail. This was not a practical solution; in a Startup Review Case study, Deepak Thomas writes that this was fraught with file-size restriction issues, unless the user was paying a premium for his or her account. Even then, there were many problems involved, such as incompatible media players, and missing codecs.[4]

In line with the flagship trends of Web 2.0, Hurley, Chen, and Karim had in mind a video-sharing site that created and facilitated *dialogue*. In other words, before 2005, even though video clips were definitely available throughout the Internet on personal websites and peer-to-peer networks, there lacked a communication between owner and user. A user, for instance, could conduct a title search and download the desired video off a website, but there being no opportunity for feedback—the relationship between the user and the website would end there. Karim also mentions that there was a lack of communication between video clips; before You-Tube, online videos remained as isolated files, without any relevance to each other. YouTube aimed to create a simple interface that would allow users to not only search and view one user video at a time, but to also view videos that related and linked to other user videos.

The team drew their inspiration from the then popular rating website HotorNot and emerging Web 2.0 application sites such as Flickr. A photo-sharing website that started in 2004, Flickr allows users to upload, tag, and search through millions of user photos. Essentially, YouTube was to be the Flickr of digital video. Flickr was subsequently acquired by Yahoo in 2005 and now serves 51 million registered users.

Growth Stage

According to YouTube founders, work got started on YouTube on February 14, 2005, and they registered the domain name the next day. Even though for the first few months the team had a rough start, they managed to create their video-sharing site at the ideal time. They were to ride, as Streaming Magazine[5] put it, a "triple wave". One such wave was the greater availability and widespread penetration of broadband connection in the home. As bandwidth became cheaper, ad revenue could conceivably offset the price of maintaining a video-sharing site. The second factor that propelled YouTube forward was their choice to use Macromedia Flash Player 7 to encode each uploaded video. The years between 2003 and 2005 marked a considerable increase in Flash video quality, and Macromedia Flash Player 7 was the first to include both audio and video. The Flash format, being one that was available in almost every browser, offered an effective solution to the problem of incompatible media players. Now, the third wave that the creators of YouTube rode was one that had to do with demand. The year 2004 brought about a surge in what Chad Hurley has often called *clip culture* meaning a widespread demand to watch popular video clips instantaneously on the Internet.[6]

Karim and Hurley linked the beginnings of this phenomenon with several events: the accidental bearing of Janet Jackson's breast at the 2004 Super Bowl, John Stewart's appearance on the show *Crossfire*, and the December 26, 2004 Indian Ocean Tsunami. The video clips featuring Janet Jackson and John Stewart are examples of events that were shown on the television once, but were never broadcast again after. Being as popular and talked about as they were, many people who missed the events on television went online to see them. The Indian Ocean Tsunami was a disaster that was captured primarily by cell phones, which sent many people to the Internet to watch the footage. Thomas[7] notes, "distributing popular hard-to-find video clips like these was 'clearly a success factor.' " These three specific examples, however, reached their popularity peak before YouTube became public; this happened on May 15, 2005.[8]

Before YouTube's popularity spiked late in 2005, in an effort to promote themselves, Chad Hurley, Steve Chen, and Jawed Karim e-mailed their friends to let them know about the site they had created. This created an initial user base, though there was not yet much draw for what they were offering. However, in June 2005, they revamped their site. They began to encourage user interaction and implemented a feature that would skyrocket the size of their website: HTML embeds.[9] This HTML code allowed users to have YouTube videos appear on their own site. Unexpectedly, this became immensely popular with Myspace users and gave YouTube a much larger base—so much that Myspace blocked video links to YouTube for a while before giving in to user pressure.[10]

In a recap of YouTube's startup, Kristin Edelhauser writes of former PayPal CFO and partner of the Venture Capitalist firm Sequoia Capital, Roelof Botha, as having a big hand in fulfilling YouTube's increasing need for an influx of cash. Edelhauser explains that after having run into Steven Chen at a party in 2005, Botha started adding personal clips to YouTube and using the service. Noting the surge in popularity that the site was receiving, Botha began to "look at it from an investor's perspective."[11] On November 7, 2005, Sequoia invested $3.5 million in private equity funding to YouTube Inc. Five months later, they invested an additional $8 million. At the time of Sequoia's initial investment, there were other venture capitalist firms looking into YouTube, however, Chad Hurley felt that Sequoia got what their site was all about and the long-lasting ties between the founders and Roelof Botha was encouraging.

Viral Video

After the $11 million VC investment into the site, Chad Hurley started implementing promotions, such as a daily iPod Nano giveaway for several months. This proved to increase their user base effectively. However, the circulation of immensely popular viral video hits seemed to be what was fueling the increase in usage of the site. For example, when YouTube hosted a skit from NBC's Saturday Night Live, "Lazy Sunday," it became a cultural sensation. The clip was originally free to download from iTunes in December 2005, and it soon circulated throughout the Internet via e-mail and YouTube. It was viewed more than 5 million times on You-Tube alone, before NBC had it removed. This particular example, along with episodes of The Office that were being uploaded, brought copyright infringement issues to the minds of large media corporations.

Chad Hurley notes that it was not copyrighted material that was most popular. Rather, the users themselves took center stage. One example that Hurley gives is Lisa Donovan, a Californian actor who uploaded a skit onto YouTube in 2006.[12] Her uploaded comedy clips featured her satirizing the likes of Rush Limbaugh and Keira Knightly; she received over 11 million views combined. Recognizing her fan-base, MADtv soon signed her for four episodes. In an article that Hurley wrote for Forbes, he elaborates on the relationship that is forming between forward-thinking media companies and web users.

User Demographics

Already in the summer of 2006 users were uploading over 65,000 videos to YouTube daily. In the month of June alone, users watched roughly 2.5 billion clips. With just over 30 employees, the site was ranked fifth most popular website on Alexa.com, and was considered the fastest growing website in the history of the Internet. According to Nielson and Netratings, during that summer, YouTube had roughly 20 million visitors each month. For its first several years, YouTube carried a cultural association with youth; however, a study done by Hitwise.com shows this to be true only in the case of viewing the site's content. During the study, only 0.16 percent of YouTube visits were related to video uploads, and only 1.9 percent of those were by 18- to 24-year-olds. On the other hand, 35.6 percent of video uploads are reportedly done by users aged 25 to 34, and 35.6 percent by users aged 35 to 44.

Google's Acquisition

In October 2006, Google acquired YouTube for $1.65 billion in stock. At the time of the deal, YouTube was getting roughly 13 million unique viewers per month and streaming an average of 100 million videos per day. The arrangement was such that Google would focus on the technological aspects of the site, while the YouTube team would continue focusing on content. Google Video and YouTube remain as separate entities, though Google includes YouTube videos in its search. Hurley has said that it was a question of growth. With the site growing as fast as it was, they needed more resources to continue. On the topic of the exit Hurley told a BBC reporter: "we didn't want features to slow down. We wanted to continue forward . . . looking at our growth, and looking at what we needed to do, we needed more resources to continue to build a great product for our users." Google's infrastructure is expected to help as digital video quality increases and needs to be encoded at "higher and multiple bit rates."[13]

The deal demonstrated that YouTube was a worthwhile investment for those initially involved and for Sequoia Capital. From the arrangement, Chad Hurley received 694,087 shares of Google and an additional 41,232 in a trust. His shares are worth more than $429 million (based on the closing price of $583.82 on February 1, 2012). Steven Chen received 625,366 shares and 68,721 in a trust, worth over $405 million. Jawed Karim, who left YouTube before the acquisition to pursue a graduate degree in computer science, received nevertheless 137,443 shares worth more than $80 million. According to the *New York Times*, Sequoia earned 941,027 shares, worth roughly $549 million. Thomas Deepak feels that Google's acquisition of YouTube falls in line nicely with their strategy of converting user visits into advertising revenue. In 2010, Google announced that YouTube was bringing in an additional $3.5 billion in revenue.[14]

Copyright Infringement, "Claim Your Content," and Revenue-Sharing

At the time of Google's acquisition, 30 to 40 percent of YouTube's content was copyrighted. Ever since YouTube's popularity began to reach unprecedented heights, people have begun to wonder is it going to be the next Napster, and end up reduced to obscurity after a hail of lawsuits.

To combat the almost certain copyright infringement lawsuits that come with the territory of sharing video content, YouTube has been partnering with major media companies. In August 2006, Hurley signed a deal with Warner Music, which allowed YouTube to host every music video produced by Warner while agreeing to share a portion of their advertising revenue. It also allowed Warner to have videos removed that they felt violated copyright laws. This was the first of many similar deals to come. Hurley recently stated that they have "well over 1,000 partnerships with outfits such as the BBC, the NBA and Sundance Channel, each of which makes use of YouTube as a platform for distribution, promotion and monetization while reaching a vast new audience."

Google developed a "Claim Your Content" program in 2006. The system is designed to automatically detect copyrighted material and remove it from the site—it also allows for users to flag content that infringes copyright. This would include such material as audio tracks in home videos. Hurley has insisted that the removal of professional copyrighted material will not harm YouTube's popularity, as what people want to see "is themselves."

As with all of the major early Web 2.0 leaders, YouTube's marketing model has been in a perpetual state of evolution. While the sites creators and major media companies are entering into partnerships that seem to hold great symbiotic promise, YouTube is also entering into very similar partnerships with the user community. On May 3, 2007, the YouTube team announced that it would be elevating the status of its most popular users to partners. This means that those favorite YouTube members, whose content has become attractive to advertisers, will participate in the same revenue sharing and promotional opportunities as YouTube's commercial partners. Essentially, after communicating with the user, YouTube will place advertisements adjacent to the user's video clips and share the advertising revenue that is generated.

Here It Goes: Blending YouTube with Brand Awareness

For several years now, companies have been using YouTube to market their product outside of paid advertisements. A great example of this is the home appliance firm BlendTec. They started posting short funny video clips on YouTube which unexpectedly took off and flooded their website with traffic. BlendTec's video series, "Will It Blend?" is a collection of clips of CEO Tom Dickenson performing "extreme blending" with their company's blenders. These low-budget clips soon became viral hits and gave BlendTec an unprecedented amount of business. The company's marketing manager, George Wright said in an interview that the results eclipsed BlendTec's expectations, "both in impact, volume and timeframe. The return for the $50 that [they] spent to produce the first round of videos is staggering." After that initial 50 dollar investment, BlendTec started receiving 6 million hits to their website every five days. They literally built a brand name for themselves through YouTube's open platform.

The indie pop quartet Ok Go, under Capitol records had a similar viral success through YouTube. The band had moderate success with their second album, "Oh No," but when it started to lose steam, they decided to privately upload a low-budget music video for their single "Here it Goes Again."[15] The video was done essentially as a joke, and featured the four band members performing an elaborately choreographed dance on eight treadmills. However, the off-the-wall music video became an instant YouTube classic and took off. The video was viewed by over a million people within its first week and was viewed over 42 million times in the next year. As the home-made video cracked YouTube's top-10 most popular videos list, Capitol jumped on booking Ok Go on the *Colbert Report* and *The Tonight Show with Jay Leno*. They won the best short-form music video Grammy for their viral success in 2007. The band's singer, Damien Kulash told *USA Today*, "I could not have dreamed of a weirder world, where the highest of top brass at our label and parent company are going, like, 'Can you guys do something really low-fi in your backyard again?' "[16] While the band will not receive royalties for their YouTube videos, it has given them a widespread audience that otherwise would probably not have been possible.

YouTube versus the Television Industry

Without a strong financial model backing YouTube, it did not appear to pose much of a threat to anybody until it's exit with Google. However, "with Google", says media consultant Tom Wolzien, "YouTube will have that model."[17] Some feel that the Google–YouTube merger gave Internet video the ability to grow claws, at least from a television standpoint.

The television industry takes in somewhere in the area of $70 billion in ad revenue annually. Estimates from 2007 saw online video taking in near $2.5 billion in revenue by 2010. Indeed, Futuresource Consulting group tracked 2011 revenues for online video sites at over $3 billion. The same report predicts the industry to grow to $7 billion by 2015.[18] While this may not seem like very stiff competition, such numbers are influencing the television industry, in areas as substantial as content and production costs.[19]

However, this is not the end of television. We are seeing that homes are accessing video on demand in addition to premium television services. Deloitte predicts that "by the end of 2014, up to 50 million homes around the world will have two or more separate pay-television subscriptions with the additional subscriptions generating about $5 Billion in revenue."[20] The introduction of new online services, such as Hulu, Vimeo, and Netflix, have forced traditional media companies to experiment with new methods of licensing and distribution. Deloitte predicts that this trend will continue. At the end of 2013, ComScore reports that people in America alone watched about 725,000 minutes of online video alone.

Discovery Questions

1. Using YouTube as its own channel for distribution is most effective when (a) the video can tap into existing online conversations and subcultures, and (b) the video has enough appeal to go viral on its own. Otherwise, YouTube can be used as a platform to host video and embed it in other channels, like your company blog, Facebook, Twitter, or some other social forum. Do you know what the best channel is to distribute video content for your company?

2. Are you comfortable with users commenting on your video content? Do you have the resources to monitor the comments section to engage and answer questions?

3. Do you have a clear goal for your video content? Do you have the resources to execute it well?

CHAPTER 9

Social Learning

Roots of Social Learning

Social learning is a paradigm that suggests that we learn, not just as a response to stimuli and reinforced by reward or punishment, but in the context of social interaction.[1] Originally developed as a response to behaviorist psychology and a model used to inform pedagogy, social learning is now an integral part of Web 2.0.[2] Social psychologists, like Lev Vygotsky and Albert Bandura, suggest that we learn best when we learn with others. Vygotsky's research found that we get better at something by working alongside someone that has a higher proficiency in a skill than we do,[3] while Bandura outlined a multistage learning hierarchy: attention, retention, reproduction, and motivation.[4] The barebones idea is that social learning occurs when we "learn with and from others."[5]

As our imaginations grew, social learning moved beyond a formal learning setting like the classroom. Early 1990s' chat applications, like ICQ[6] and MSN Messenger,[7] provided a prototype for future collaboration tools by allowing users to interact, send files, and store transcripts of conversations. Essentially, instant messaging was the first iteration of an online social network that forms the backbone of social learning. The introduction of social media in the late 1990s and early 2000s changed the way we communicated, and although organizations originally saw these tools as a marketing opportunity, they were eventually reframed as a way to spread organizational knowledge and expertise community-wide.[8] So, with the incorporation of social media, the term social learning went from a pedagogical paradigm to an action-oriented organizational strategy.

Major Market Players

1993 Aviation Industry Computer-Based Training Committee (AICC) produced what is widely regarded as the first run time interoperability specification for learning management systems.

1995 First Wiki page appeared online at c2.com—*wikiwikiweb* by Ward Cunningham.

1996 First widely adapted GUI instant messenger application is released—ICQ leads the market in instant messaging technology.

1996 Courseinfo LLC releases "Teacher Toolbox" a web application for developing courses and quizzes.

1997 Courseinfo LLC and Blackboard LLC joined to form Blackboard Inc., who would become the authority in online social learning.

1997 Saba Software was founded, providing enterprise talent management cloud solutions.

1999 Desire2Learn Founded and release their learning management system.

2000 Sharable Content Object Reference Model (SCORM) Version 1.0 was released; a specification of the Advanced Distributed Learning (ADL) Initiative, which comes out of the Office of the United States Secretary of Defense.

2001 SuccessFactors founded in California, starts providing a cloud-based LMS.

2004 SumTotal Systems started offering its LMS as part of its Human Resources solutions.

2011 CoursePeer founded and started offering Social LMS and MOOC to academia, then expanded to offer enterprise LMS, Collaboration and Decision-Making solutions.

The Early Years—Wiki's and the Collaborative Web

Tracing the formation of social learning as it relates to Web 2.0 becomes difficult because it is really an amalgamation and reframing of several web technologies. Moving beyond its components (instant messaging, social media, content database), the first real instance of social learning online was the development of *wikiwikiweb* at C2.com. In 1994, Ward Cunningham uploaded the first wiki, about programming patterns to his domain C2.com. Ward describes a wiki as

> content before community. Low latency to correction. The work-flow of submission starts with publication—publish and then edit. Trivial creation of new pages, to let them grow to the right size. And a community provided by recent changes—the ability to see what other editors are doing, encouraging visitors to go from readers to authors to editors.[9]

In his book "The *Wiki Way: Quick Collaboration on the Web*" Ward and coauthor Bo Leuf characterize a wiki as: an open platform that promotes the meaningful association of pages, *wiki pages*, into an almost living document grown by many authors. Essentially, Ward's idea and implementation of *the wiki* was the first online collaborative document without barriers to editing. This idea would be carried over into the social learning model used by learning management system providers and passed onto organizations looking to augment their training with an online social learning component.[10]

Although the collaboration element was there, the editing of online wikis lacked the real-time, interactive social networking component that now forms the backbone of modern social learning. What it did do well was allow subject matter experts to work collaboratively, while sharing their knowledge with a wider online audience. Bringing together learners and subject matter experts within an organization became a crucial component to the structure of the modern learning management systems on the market today.

The Adolescent Years—The Rise of Learning Management Systems

Between 1997 and 2000, during the dot-com bubble, Blackboard Inc. was founded and would go on to be the most successful learning management company in the Education Tech (EdTech) market.[11] This was the start of the learning management systems rise to the forefront of the online learning revolution. The learning management system, Blackboard Inc.'s flagship product and the most oft developed social learning tool, "is the infrastructure that delivers and manages instructional content, identifies and assesses individual and organizational learning or training goals, tracks the progress toward meeting those goals, and collects and presents data for supervising the learning process of organization as a whole."[12]

Learning management systems have become a mainstay in both the academia and the corporate world but the requirements are slightly different depending on where the system is implemented. Bailey has suggested that academic learning management systems require the following:[13]

- Learning objectives need to be tied to lessons;
- Lessons fit into a standard curriculum;
- Student performance is collected; and
- Individual student performance dictates lesson flow.

Corporate learning management systems, like those being offered by: Saba, SumTotal, SuccessFactors, and CoursePeer, tend to require a much more complex system that:[14]

- can be integrated with human resource software;
- have administrative tools (profiles, certification, learning paths);
- use blended learning;
- have skill managing; and
- adhere to SCORM standards.

The important thing to note about the adolescent years of social learning is that the learning management systems at the time had a limited social learning component. Generally, the systems offered social learning through forum-type interactions. Although forums are considered real-time interaction, they lacked the tools to collaboratively author documents, create polls, or encourage collaborative problem solving. It wasn't until the social media boom that learning management systems began to take full advantage of the power of social learning.

The Mature Years

In the era of Web 2.0, learning management systems have taken on a new life. With the rise of social media, learning management systems have harnessed the interactive qualities of Web 2.0 technologies and applied them to the learning process thereby fully embracing the social learning experience. A 2005 study found that 56 percent of young people in America were using computers for "creative activities, writing and posting of the Internet, mixing and constructing multimedia and developing their own content." Twelve to 17-year-olds look to web tools to share what they think and do online. One in five who use the net said they used other people's images, audio or text to help make their own creations.[15]

Before the revitalization of the learning management systems on the market, they didn't take advantage of these elements. That's all changed. learning management systems have now implemented technology that allows users to interact in a new way. Using a social media-like back-end has allowed companies, such as Blackboard Inc., Desire2Learn, and CoursePeer, to implement functionalities that include:

- customizable profiles;
- user-generated content feeds;
- ability to share multi-media content;
- collaborative authoring; and
- collaborative problem-solving tools.

With these tools in place, and more ways of working together being developed constantly, social learning has now been integrated into Web 2.0 learning management systems.

What's Next?

Various EdTech incubators and accelerators have emerged in 2013, investing in and supporting EdTech entrepreneurs. Enterprise is more interested nowadays in adopting successful learning approaches from Academia and three of the main trends emerging in enterprise recently are game-based learning, Massive Open Online Courses (MOOC) and the shift from one-size-fits-all learning to a more personalized one.

With employees naturally spending their time on social networks, enterprise social learning platforms started partnering with content creators providing interactive games to deliver a more engaging knowledge transfer mechanism, which makes learners more entertained while getting the knowledge they need to perform their jobs. And with MOOCs becoming more interesting to enterprise learning leaders, organizations are starting to consider publishing some of their best practices on the social web as public courses, as well as allowing employees from any department to access such course catalogs, whenever they want.

With analytics and big data being another trend in enterprise HR, education technology solutions are focusing more on empowering trainers with analytics dashboards. This allows learning and HR leaders to improve their training programs based on feedback they get around the consumption of courses, as well as the social interactions around their training programs. CoursePeer Inc., for example, is one of the companies that has patented technology that allows administrators of such systems to easily visualize, as well as program learning content around analytics which provides a more personalized learning environment for employees, leveraging the concept of pushing useful and interesting training content to the audience without them needing to search for it. Such analytical measures include passion, engagement, and sentiment.

The future is very promising for social learning and collaboration tools as the industry has matured to recognize that talent development is critical to human performance. As the war for talent accelerates, companies must continue to implement social learning solutions that give them a competitive edge.

Discovery Questions

1. Do learning management systems have a place in the modern organization?
2. How could your organization use social learning or collaborative tools to create a competitive advantage?

CHAPTER 10

Social Prospecting

Introduction[1]

Social prospecting takes the discipline of sales strategies developed over the past one hundred years and utilizes new methods of identifying buying signals to connect with customers in preferred channels of communication. It is traditional outreach, coupled with the power of social media, to evolve how listening and communication can impact the sales process in the context of people.[2]

Today, sales teams have evolved to be a more dynamic customer-centric team, focusing on sales at many levels of the buying cycle. These diverse interactions from multiple sources increase pressure to connect with future customers as early as possible. The competitive landscape is pervasive with innovative technologies focused on business process rather than IT infrastructure. The end result is that process innovation has produced a plethora of new sales techniques over the past two decades. Today, the focus is on developing relationships grounded in authentic behavior to cultivate a long-term mutually beneficial relationship, and removing the decades of sales methods such as canvassing and the infamous door-to-door prospecting that in today's modern age is not the sales pathway for customer connection. To get to win, sales leaders must embrace social prospecting approaches to be successful.

Social prospecting is an evolution from the former traditional models of leveraging phone or e-mail interactions to use social networks to optimize relationship connections.

Roots of Social Prospecting

Over the past decade, technology has changed the landscape and the skills expected from the everyday sales and marketing professional, impacting their approach in developing and qualifying sales strategies and tactics.

This fundamental shift occurred when technology-driven solutions began optimizing the data sets retrieved from Web activities. These new data sets paved the way to the new modern marketer to form the discipline that many pioneers in the industry categorized as marketing automation, which tracks data from Web activity and correlates the information in a similar context within e-mails that gave sales teams and marketers a faster way to identify customer persona (i.e., buyer profiles). These new insights have led to modernizing sales funnel engagement touch points or interactions often called, the cascade effect, or as defined in this chapter as social prospecting.

The industry has been maturing in evolving enterprise sales solution methodologies from proven sales selling practices driven from Xerox, and defined by Michael Bosworth as Solution Selling.[3] Since its inception in 1984, this de facto solution selling methodology focused on the repeatability of a sale based on focusing on customer needs and pain points, while also leveraging technology or product capabilities into a solution offering. The root of solution selling, originally founded through the sales practices of Xerox, paved the way to enable sales and marketing professionals to position customer solutions in more comprehensive, applicable, and sustainable ways than ever before.

With the constant advancements in technology, digital and web-centric innovations are in continual year-over-year growth, creating new verticals, while enhancing segments of the sales processes and strategies. Consider the desktop computing segment, which sprung from giants, such as Microsoft, IBM, Intel, Dell, and other networking giants like Cisco. Their offerings were a product under a licensed model sold directly to the customer, typically an enterprise fixed license fee. The introduction of the World Wide Web (WWW) brought an expansion in the breadth and depth of services available and introduced new multinational web-based business players, such as eBay, Google, and Yahoo. Online web software providers have opened up the ecosystem to new revenue opportunities, while disrupting an aged service delivery model. As early as 2001, companies, such as ClubRunner, ExactTarget, Salesforce.com, and WebEx, went to market with the idea of offering enterprise-grade applications as rental software, delivered via the cloud, and coined Software as a

Service (SaaS). These companies were pioneers of delivering high-quality platform applications, fully enabled through web services. These models have challenged traditional enterprise license models (on premise), versus the off premise (or SaaS) models.[4]

Changing Landscape Impacts Sales Professional's Role

The role of the salesperson is to generate trust as an opportunity for a unique selling proposition that is required to help add value to grow a business in today's fast changing environment. As a result, the trusted salesperson becomes the driver to sales prospecting methods. Prospecting and the evolution of social networks has accelerated the engagement methods by which sales teams can proactively network with prospects or customers, and utilize social technology to facilitate a one-to-many, synchronous affect.

The Market Players

1970s IBM utilized its network of executives to promote the brand to engage new prospects.

1980 CompuServe, first online dedicated service to online chat—discussion board where invitations were sent.

1999 Amazon: focused on the customer and the early adoption of customers.

2000 Hotmail: introduction to the viral component of prospecting, came from the method Microsoft used to grow the user base.

2001 Salesforce.com: innovated sales practice tools delivered via the web.

2002 Eloqua: marketing automation, ReachLocalL live chat.

2003 ClubRunner: membership communication platform.

2008 Radian6: marketing analytics and tracking on social channels.

2009 Rapportive: Gmail inbox integrated contact social preview.

2010 OneSource: aggregated business information service.

2011 InsideView: centralized contact list and search service.

2012 realSociable: social prospecting.

The Early Years—Asynchronous Online Tools

Today, engagement and relationships can be formed easily with social transparency. The question that many technology innovators asked with the rise of Internet services and the .com era was, "How can we engage the audience visiting our web pages to capture their attention and create a connection?"

Having deeper knowledge creates the trusted role that can lead to a long-term relationship with the customer. Solving the problem-based sale of the solution and delivering a plan can lead to customer success and greater lifetime value. If a salesperson can get into the mind-set of the buyer even at the research phase, this can eliminate many lost sales cycles within cold calling and social engagements. Cold calling is one of the hardest forms of engagement, yet carries the highest rewards if the skill can be mastered. That is, he or she can walk into a new office or pick up the phone and speak with someone that he or she has no prior relation with for the purpose of setting up a meeting. In reality, this task is daunting and takes an experienced person to handle the emotional roller coaster that cold calling creates. Irrespective of the skills that sales professionals develop to prospect directly through cold calling, companies started to place gate keepers to increase the barrier of these tactics, posing a difficulty to the prospecting priority.[5]

With the evolution of cold calling came web-based customer service or sales lead generation, with onsite sales chat to assist with questions that arise when a user lands on the client's web page. This evolution paved a new way for companies, such as eBuddy and ReachLocal, which began inserting sales conversations to attract and capture a synchronous dialogue with the visitor. Unlike the traditional chat services that were originally discovered by Doug Brown and David R. Woolley in 1974 with Talkomatic,[6] which was eventually commercialized as CompuServe, this new revolution of chat was based in website interaction. This chat approach was commercialized as a widget to capture a messaging experience versus the notion of instant messaging known to many as ICQ, Windows Messenger, and Yahoo! IM.

Sales tools have evolved, such as ReachLocal's live chat platform, which provides a method to position sales or trained agents, which assists visitors as they navigate through websites creating higher sales conversion rates. This one-to-many approach helped to shape the new business networking and sales prospecting interaction methods.

The economics of the sales professional, and the cost of networking to offset the burden of prospecting in traditional one-to-one methods, have to evolve to asynchronous capabilities. Individual sales teams that focused their prospecting efforts by integrating technology-driven tactics capitalized their investments by optimizing their websites to be research tools. This further accelerated the technology evolution as social conversion ratios started to demonstrate the value of social prospecting. According to eMarketer, a digital media research firm found in 2009, 53 percent of online consumers had utilized chat in some form or another, showcasing a rapid adoption rate in this stage of prospecting. Another recent customer survey compiled by live chat software service Click4Assistance published statistics around chat and online commerce and discovered that 43 percent of visitors would have left the website entirely if an instant chat option wasn't available to them. This new method of web prospecting gained traction in many disciplines and became a foundational element to evolve web-enabled communication services.

The Adolescent Years—Automated Human and the Advent of MultiChannels

As the economics of effective prospecting, using singular tactics such as online chat, networking events, or even listings, gained market adoption, a shift emerged to focus on sales tactics that had demonstrated conversion metrics, With the advent of technology-based analytics and multiple online methods to capture the prospecting dialogue marketers and sales teams began shifting their attention to the notion of ROI for sales prospecting technology investments. Conversion rate metrics proved to be the indicator focusing more on improving site flow, online customer service channels, and online experiences.[7]

Another shift began with technology-driven tools, focusing on the process of different communication channels that proved to have high prospecting yields and the ability to utilize technology business processes to automate. The overarching extension of such a multifaceted platform driven by high-powered mission-critical software was established by the extension of customer relationship management (CRM). According to a Sweeney Group definition,[8] CRM is "all the tools, technologies and procedures to manage, improve, or facilitate sales, support and related interactions with customers, prospects, and business partners throughout the enterprise."

The push for growth and the scale of ROI helped remove barrier to engaging prospects and accelerated the value of the long tail effect. Usage of asynchronous tools pushed the boundaries of multichannel strategies, particularly as the adoption of e-mail messaging was now a mainstream business practice. The automation of sales and marketing communications intensified web-centric human interactions and automated the process using technology to push out process protocols en masse. CRM emerged from a back-office system to a customer-centric communication process across organizations enabling particular teams to manage multitouch communication approaches and campaigns while tracking in CRM. This shift and the dialogue of campaigns management began to be seen as common phrase even in most business-to-business (B2B) environments. As barriers to entry reduced and innovation occurred in technology and e-mail communication systems, it became prevalent in day-to-day modern business that a new wave of multichannel, high-volume prospecting methods was reaching maturity.

Automation and the advent of e-mail marketing in CRM now deconstructed the traditional business process of prospecting, which enabled a process flow to be operated by a marketing generalist simulating the notion of a larger team increasing conversion rates and the top line growth of a company's bottom line. The new CRM web-enabled customer or prospect interaction tracking services became a de facto practice and modernized the role of the sales and marketing professionals. Having the capability to track, engage, qualify, in some degree, was a breadcrumb scenario that prospecting tactics couldn't do before. This online breadcrumb effect and the ability to construct the ideal conversation through a digital framework was also broken down into the phrase *digital body language* as Steve Woods, cofounder of Eloqua, states in Digital Body Language, a criterion to begin an overall storytelling campaign to prospects requires the need to consistently interact with contacts in the form of e-mail and corporate messaging exposing this new multidimensional sales prospecting approach.[9] Although a necessary part of the sales process and the marketing funnel's requirement to generate demand, it has also caused pressure for sales teams to convert at the same rate of generating awareness, and the nuance of effective conversion became a challenge. This generic messaging needs an interruption, as it is taking away the genuineness and authenticity from the engaged sales team. Now, a decade into the innovation of CRM automation solutions (that support sales and marketing demands), the next generation, the mature years, of early adopters are discovering unique signals that are outside the organization's assets and ultimately push the qualification cycle to increasing external engagement interactions.

The Mature Years—Technology Focusing on the Human-to-Human Interactions

Today's sales environment relies heavily on the usage of CRM, which creates automation of data and contact insights, while building a sales funnel. The new social media revolution is delivering a competitive advantage to sales organizations looking to decouple old methodologies and adopt new forms of engagement. Contrary to common perceptions, sales representatives gaining customer traction are not necessarily those via Facebook and Twitter. Social networking applications are enabling a new method of qualification and prospecting that extends outside of a company's assets such as web pages or tradeshow floors. Profiling techniques began with companies such as Rapportive (now a LinkedIn entity), which identified social networks associated with a specific customer.

Social networks have revolutionized the workforce by augmenting how sales and marketing teams communicate and collaborate with customers. With new tools to manage social conversations, organizations can be more affective at listening to social media mentions related to their specific brands. Industry leaders in social management like Radian6 have created a baseline for industry to understand customer conversations and help evaluate how to engage appropriately. Social media management applications have enabled companies to listen to the back channels of social networks (i.e., Twitter for different keywords for the purpose of customer service and simple prospecting methods). These approaches have proved successful and sales teams who had resources to have this managed in their groups began to see the benefit of having a current view of their prospecting landscape. However, it's not enough for companies to just to have a presence on Twitter and Facebook without having a cohesive *social intelligence* strategy.

A badly designed and dissonant communication process disrupts the effective flow of communication and intended messaging and leads to a sluggish audience response. This in turn contributes to a negative experience and engagement between a company and their clients and subscribers.

Social networks are creating more competitive, connected, and collaborative companies; they are helping groups come together and accomplish more with less effort. Alternatively, it is those who understand how to utilize their online social networks in order to grow their sales. Through fragmentation and industry alignment, new companies, like Inside View, IntroHive, and realSociable, in the forefront as thought leaders on how to consume smarter data, while building strategic direction for companies on their engagements. One of the more innovative companies is realSociable, which views the social integration into CRM as a seamless component, applying logic to the different touch points. The feeds available from social media provide insights that sales representatives can use to acquire customers—the approach of this method realSociable calls this, Perpetual Prospecting.™ Social media has the potential to empower the enterprise user, enabling the enterprise to be in touch with their client's digital landscape, and understand the client's requirements and needs by amassing rich data sources of insight.

It is imperative for companies to embrace social media tools and best practices to apply to their businesses to take advantage of the benefits from applying perpetual prospecting. The dynamics and characteristics of enterprise social media are distinct from that of the consumer environment. The latter has a higher emphasis on engaging from an outbound method, taking a social prospecting strategy requires commitment from an organization with a goal to engage proactively.

A high-profile example is Cisco's social strategy. Although they have had many years of empowering their marketing team to social practices, once they made the decision to extend this across their sales funnel and extract a simpler way of sharing this to the day-to-day process that their sales teams live by, they saw a significant increase to their sales. Although the Cisco team didn't realize the impact of breaking this down, it was something they had to see as the influence on any conversation had the potential to sway decisions that had a significant value to the organization. Charlie Treadwell, Cisco's social intelligence manager led the initiative all the way. "We had started by listening to our customers' conversations, identifying their pain points in an effort to guide our objectives," says Treadwell, formerly an art director in Cisco corporate affairs, who was charged with monetizing the social listening experiment. "Management started saying, 'the honeymoon is over. We need to show value.' "[10]

The focus was to cut the response time, and place less reaction and build a responsive culture across the board. Not only did Cisco's success pave the way for social prospecting methods, but it also showcased the variance of how consumer-like publishing and outbound means were not enough and were not the shear responsibility of a marketing team, for any size organization. Cisco, after its first year of completion, not only credits for achieving a higher response time, deeper communications, and higher sales, but it also boasted an overall 281 percent ROI to the impact it has had in its sales group.[11]

The success social prospecting can bear on an organization can be dramatically realized if the notion of leveraging social media applications is truly understood to be focused on engagement and not the traditional idea of publishing. The casual application of consumer-oriented social media practices can be entirely inappropriate and ineffective in an enterprise environment. Building tactical objectives ranging from pipeline development to brand management while growing and reinforcing your company's champions are part of a strategic move into sociable communication tools.

Companies are integrating and embracing social media tools at a faster rate than e-mail took off back in the 1990s, as it is becoming an integral part of their communication and content strategies. This will continue to be a sustainable competitive advantage relative to their socially impeded counterparts. However, this inherently requires more than a passive approach to social media where community managers post content and sales teams casually trawl for information. A truly effective social media strategy proactively and constructively integrates social media in all aspects of the company's organization and processes.

This phase of integrating technology to produce singular yet human interaction capabilities provides context into each conversation made by sales members and communities. This approach is building a genuine conversation, which relates to the customer without focusing on their business, products, or corporate quotas. This approach, embraced, can yield a tremendous benefit to the bottom line, while also creating efficiency to the organization in many ways: reducing the level of internal communications to react to acquired data points, reducing the reactive time gap, and improving the overall rapport of customer relations. Similar to the Cisco example, the social interaction investments being made although early stage are creating the demonstrable proof from using new technology platforms, like realSociable, which are designed to provide a 360 degree view to enable engagement with context and relevancy.

What's Next?

Marketing teams have constantly tried to effectively segment their potential customer base to determine what messages would be best suited to the various segments.[12] Paul Hague and Matthew Harrisson's article, "Market Segmentation in B2B Markets" stresses the importance to "know your customers, know how they differ, and have a clear proposition that lights their fire."

Hague explores various criteria within B2B marketing segmentation that typically starts by looking at geography and language to communicate to their customer base within set segments, like demographics, company size, and industry. However, these segments do not give an organization the ability to truly know their customer and map a value proposition based on customer behavior and needs. As segmentation, coupled with online solutions merge with the ability to assess a profile of the customer's social footprint, the ability to imagine the persona and approach is enabling this new simpler prospecting solution to emerge, focusing on the potential as a dimension rather than the sheer metrics produced by an analytics engine. The need to use segments or personas to qualify and prioritize enables social prospecting and presents golden nuggets to sales teams—one at a time, human to human.

The ROI that matters the most is the investment made by a team crafting, developing, and nurturing relationships with customers and potential clients. This shift of placing humans back in control of their conversations is a resonance of the techniques first utilized in the modern era of marketing agencies and solution selling. Some might say that it's about metrics and seeing a particular number pop up at the end of a campaign. That's true enough, but when it comes right down to it, prospecting is about people doing business with people, and the connection made as early as possible tends to indicate the strength of that relationship.

In summary, the new customer-centric sales teams who take advantage of social prospecting methodologies will enable their teams with more comprehensive data at their fingertips. This data is giving an individual and the team the ability to be always aware, thereby creating new opportunities to qualify and disqualify sales opportunities. Intent and interest is a powerful engagement and connection agent to advance and create the shortest path to sales goal achievement. According to Gordon, an expert in sales innovation, the time is now for sales professionals to embrace social prospecting, customers are spending more time in social channels, and less interaction time is spent on phone, e-mail contact points, so social prospecting is not a new way. It is now the most optimal way to get to win.[13]

Discovery Questions

1. What tools are your sales representatives using to gain customer traction?
2. What segments offer the greatest potential for social prospecting?
3. Does your sales organization use any social media engagement tools for sales branding?
4. How much time do your sales professional(s) spend researching prior to making a customer call? What if they had the ability to have the customer updates come to them in real time, and be alerted to customer interaction moments?
5. What are the benefits that you can see from using social prospecting methods to change your business?

CHAPTER 11

Social Analytics

The Challenge

We have discussed the root stories of social media giants throughout this book that have transformed the digital landscape. The rapid rise of social media and online communications has been blurring the division between social and traditional marketing, market research, PR, advertising, CRM, customer services, and even innovation. Social approaches are now infusing all companies' business practices, processes, and activities. Companies are increasingly investing into social media programs and purchasing social media monitoring technologies and services to help develop their strategies. They are being integrated into core business operations—and simply like we experienced having telephone in the office we now have social in the office—this is just how we now work. The fact some companies are still questioning the value is simply resulting in lost time to connect with their customers in channel they prefer to be talked in.

We have had a plethora of diverse social media networking giants alter the digital landscape. As important as Facebook, or Google, or Twitter, or Blogger, or LinkedIn are in advancing our social media experiences, what is equally important is understanding what value these interaction patterns have in creating business value.

In other words, irrespective of the social noise in the Web, companies must also answer questions such as the following:

- How many people are reading or looking at your social content?
- Where is the real value coming from? (i.e., how many incoming calls have come in from social channels that convert into customer purchases?)
- How can we improve our operational practices as a result of social insights?

- How can we influence the positive social patterns to grow our businesses?
- How do we leverage our social investments to achieve a positive ROI?

Many companies today are still struggling with what is the value question in using social approaches to solve business challenge. Although we have provided numerous examples throughout this book on the value of social approaches, we wanted to bring our readers additional insights on social measurement, based on key market leaders, and share some leading practices.

Social Media Analytics—Defined

According to Wikipedia, social analytics was developed in the early 1980s by the Danish philosopher Lars-Henrik Schmidt. The theoretical object of the perspective is *socius*, a kind of commonness that is neither a universal account nor a communality shared by every member of a body.[1]

Social media analytics is best defined as the measurement and the analysis of interactions and associations between people, topics, and ideas using social channels. Social media analytics is a powerful tool for uncovering customer sentiment dispersed across diverse web centric sources. Social media analytics allow marketing, sales, and customer service professionals to identify consumer or customer behavior trends to understand the customer better. Social media analytics or monitoring tools typically assist organizations to:

- acquire insights in support of how their social marketing campaigns and communication plans are doing and provide statistical information on number of views, linkages of social patterns back to purchasing events;
- enable greater insights into the behavior, sentiment, and effectiveness of marketing and communication efforts, by mining data into terms of age, gender, languages, geography, and so forth;
- support content and engagement strategies to improve the promotion of products and services;

- engage in a customer service issue online; or
- discuss a product or solution using social for sales prospecting engagement.

Social Media Players—Time Line

2001 Lithium Technologies spin out from GX Media, launches social experience management platform.

2002 Sysomos social media monitoring launches.

2004 Google Analytics launches.

2007 Topsy launches providing instant answers and a search engine on social trends.

2008 Hootsuite was founded by Canadian, Ryan Holmes.

2010 Sysomos is acquired by MarketWire.

2011 SalesForce.com buys Radiant 6 for $326 million and starts acquired social analytic companies.

2013 Apple buys social media monitoring Topsy for $200 million.

2013 Lithium Technologies announces its plans to go public in a pre-IPO offering.

2014 Lithium Technologies purchases Klout for $100 million.

2014 SalesChoice launches—Sales Predictions Suite (Big Data social media B2B).

2014 HootSuite acquires uberVu.

Social Media—Getting Started, Simplified View

The first step in a social media analytics initiative is to identify what the business goals are, determine the questions that need answering, identify where the data sources are in social channels relevant to achieving the goals, answering the questions, setting up a process to execute effectively, and analyze the benefits. Typical goals framing social media programs using analytics are:

- improving customer experience, providing an alternative customer service channel to provide a feedback loop or voice to the company;

- gaining new customer insights on products or services;
- identifying engagement pathways to increase sales and top line growth;
- reducing customer service costs, and
- improving public opinion of a particular product or business division.

These are some of the goals that we often see in our client projects. What is important to understand is that social media is an opportunity to engage more directly with customers online in a channel that they often prefer to use.

Once the business goals have been identified, key performance indicators (KPIs) need to be defined. This helps to translate what outcomes you are targeting to evaluate by defining the specific metrics that you will track to gain the insights that you are seeking to achieve. For example, customer engagement might be measured by the following:

- The numbers of followers of a Facebook or a Twitter account.
- The numbers of retweets and mentions of a company's name.
- Tracking the number and type of social media channels that converts to a sales rep successfully booking a customer call.
- Number of customer service or sales calls that converts to a new customer purchase.
- Following customer usage patterns of social to predict new product or service innovation(s).

There are also a number of types of software tools for analyzing unstructured data found in tweets and Facebook posts. In addition to text analysis, many enterprise-level social media tools will harvest and store the data.

The next section explores some of the early and adolescent market players that are making a major impact on the social analytics space, including Google Analytics and Hootsuite. We will close with a future perspective predictive analytics and how this approach will also evolve the social analytics market landscape.

Google Analytics: Early Market Player

Google Analytics has its roots in a company called Web Depot. Web Depot developed a tool in 1998 called Urchin, designed to process website tracking information efficiently and quickly. At the time, processing that kind of data typically took around 24 hours, but Urchin was able to do it in 15 minutes. This kind of improvement on existing capabilities was enough to convince the team to pivot away from consulting and focus on Urchin.

Urchin cofounder Paul Muret writes about the response to the first rollout of Urchin: "It was clear that Urchin was filling a fundamental need to understand customer engagement in a new medium. Suddenly, it made the intangible packets of traffic flying invisibly all over the world very tangible."[2] The company soon after became Urchin Software Corporation. "Our philosophy was always to create a product that was fairly simple to get going and didn't require a tremendous amount of technical support," says Brett Cosby, cofounder of Urchin Software and current Director of Product Marketing at Google.[3] "We built our business around a very scalable product, which allowed us to do things like target hosting companies and get massive numbers of users with one deal, rather than focusing on one very complex deal."[4]

What differentiated Urchin was that the software operated on a hybrid approach to data collection: it pulled from both web server log files and page tag beacons, resulting in much greater accuracy than was available on the market at the time.[5]

Urchin launched a SaaS version of their product in 2004 called Urchin-on-Demand. The price tag for this service started at $500 per month.[6] This version did not rely on server-side log files, but operated on page tagging. Brian Clifton writes that he gave more independence to marketers to perform web measurements without having to involve IT beyond the initial set-up.[7] Urchin-on-demand was also an improvement for companies that used Google AdWords, as it allowed marketers to now run improved marketing reports.[8]

Google approached Urchin in 2004 and acquired the company in 2005. At the time, Urchin was reporting that its customers included NBC, NASA, and AT&T and "a fifth of the Fortune 500."[9] In 2005, it was estimated that the acquisition was worth $30 million. Several months after the acquisition, Google rolled out Google Analytics, which would bring analysis and understanding of web traffic and behavior to millions of Internet users. It would also allow Google Ads and AdWords services to be bolstered by real numbers and analysis.

Google launched Google Analytics in November 2005. Unlike Urchin and Urchin-on-demand, Google Analytics was free. Deep web analytics were free for everyone on the web for the first time—the impact of this was huge. Clifton writes, "an industry that once counted its customers in the tens of thousands, now exploded. In fact so dramatic was the uptake of the service that it had to close to new subscribers for 10 months while new machines were allocated to the number crunching tasks at Google's data centers . . . once re-opened, the user base of Google Analytics rapidly expanded beyond a million in a matter of months."[10]

HootSuite: Adolescent Market Player

Vancouver-based Hootsuite has been one of Canada's biggest social media success stories in the past decade. The service has roughly 7 million users and has proven to be a valuable tool for companies managing social media feeds and communities. Their primary service is to manage multiple social channels from the same online platform. As the company has grown, the value of their analytics components has become more apparent. By combining multiple social channels into one, Hootsuite has the ability to synthesize valuable insights for its users. This is the kind of space where big data becomes really truly big.

Hootsuite was originally built as an in-house app by a marketing company called Invoke Media. The tool was developed to help the small company manage multiple Twitter accounts simultaneously for their clients. It was originally named Brightkit and the team released its tool publically at the end of November 2008. In the Brightkit launch announcement, marketing coordinator Kate LeGresley explains that existing tools like Tweetdeck and thwirl did not meet their needs. On top of general functionality tweaks, they felt a need for a scheduler and URL shortener. Meet BrightKit—the ultimate Twitter toolbox:.

> BrightKit lets you manage multiple Twitter profiles and pre-schedule tweets. . . . BrightKit will provide solid tweet metrics

right on the dashboard, and loads of additional features are on the way. We've even created one of the most succinct URL shorteners on the market, ow.ly, a little homage to the BrightKit Owl.[11]

The URL shortener "ow.ly" is what would make Hootsuite an important story in the development of social analytics. As simply a Twitter toolbox, Brightkit would be limited to Twitter metrics. However, with a URL shortener, the company had fast access to click-through rates and a greater sense of reach.

The initial metrics available through ow.ly click-throughs were in line with traditional marketing techniques, such as traffic flow, A/B testing, different copy, and the impact of sending out messages at different times of day. For Hootsuite, this was about tracking the path from social media to purchase, thereby connecting social media and ROI.

Quite shortly after the release of Brightkit, Invoke caught the eye of writer Adam Ostrow at Mashable. "We've seen a number of Twitter tools for scheduling future tweets, shortening URLs, and tracking click-thrus," writes Ostrow. "But BrightKit (not to be confused with the location-aware app BrightKite) is the sleekest we've seen yet, making it worth a mention." Brightkit's popularity grew quickly. By February 2009 they had roughly 100,000 users. "We built all of our own business eating our own dog food," CEO Ryan Holmes says. "We're absolute believers in social media. From day one we built community and engaged with community."[12]

The group also turned to crowdsourcing. In February, they decided to change their name, after having been contact by a similarly named company Bright Kite. "Our brand wasn't cemented, so we crowd sourced our name," Holmes says.

We asked our one hundred thousand users and asked them what they thought our name should be. We had our cute little owl mascot at that point. Someone came up with Hootsuite and it made sense right away.[13]

Shortly after changing their name, Hootsuite expanded their product's support to Facebook and LinkedIn. In 2009, they spun off from Invoke Media and became their own company.

By 2011, HootSuite had over 3 million users and operated on a freemium model. In March 2011, they launched HootSuite Social Analytics. This marked an increase in measurement and analytical tools as well as customizable report templates. On top of tracking Ow.ly stats, the platform also pulled in Facebook Insights, Google Analytics, Google+ Page Analytics, and Organizational Analytics.

In October 2012, HootSuite announced that it would be integrating with Webtrends, an analytics company.[14] The announcement revealed that an important part of their enterprise was in information. They said that this integration would provide to enterprise clients "a level of measurement consistent with search-engine marketing and display ad markets for accurate cross-channel comparisons."[15]

This integration allowed HootSuite to take their analytics to another level of sophistication. The company listed a series of questions that they knew enterprise level analytics could address. These included: "Which message types result in the highest number of conversions?" "What are the best practices for increasing specific on-site actions?", "Is there a business case to invest more resources in organic online engagement?", and "Which words drive the most conversions?"[16]

By the end of 2013, HootSuite was servicing 7 million users and had raised $165 million in series B funding. In January 2014, they announced their acquisition of social analytics leader UberVu. This acquisition has made it clear where the value of such cross-channel engagement platforms lie.

"uberVU's product is a next-generation social analytics solution that turns data from blogs, forums and social networks into actionable business insights," Holmes writes on the company blog. "uberVU helps businesses better understand their social audience by identifying key influencers on relevant topics, easily detecting real-time spikes in engagement (with insights on sentiment, location, and demographics), and highlighting important mentions." They began immediately offering uberVu's services, but will be working on closer integration of the products going forward.

The Future—The Rise of Predictive Analytics

With tremendous data volume in social media channels, the future will be very much predicated on the advancement of predictive analytics to project future outcomes. In the words of Newton's Third Law, "For every action there is an equal and opposite reaction." According to Dr. Cindy Gordon in a blog posting:

> Predictive analytics is powered by the world's most potent, booming unnatural resource: data. Accumulated in large part as the by-product of routine tasks, filling out sales funnel information, sending emails to customers, calling customers, social media conversations, etc. Data is being accumulated at staggering rates worldwide, and every day, the data mass is growing. As organizations keep churning away, unsalted, even flavorless deposits on masse, predictive analytics are looking at the big data heap as a gold mine bonanza. Big data embodies an extraordinary wealth of experience from which to learn. As our world starts to make this quantum shift, we will soon have predictive sensors everywhere and in everything. Predictive analytics unleashes the power of data. With this technology, the computer literally learns from data how to predict the future behavior of customers, individuals, and companies. Perfect prediction is not possible, but putting odds on the future—lifting a bit of the fog off our increasingly complex world that we live in. The world has simply become far too complex for us as humans to decipher. Predictive analytics is becoming big news…As predictive analytics embed more deeply into mainstream core applications in both sales and marketing processes, we will start to see improvements, which McKinsey is touting could indeed offer 10 CAGR growth rates to companies.[17]

Social Prediction Leading Researchers

The future is often embedded in the research of leading academics, unfortunately many business leaders are not mining the minds of leading academic researchers as much as they should be. MIT Professor Devavrat Shah developed a new algorithm that can, with 95 percent accuracy, predict the Twitter topics that trend, or will explode in volume, thus predicting popularity trends before they occur. Twitter determines the trending topics based on its own algorithm that analyzes the number of tweets and those that have recently grown in volume, according to an MIT report on the research.[18]

Other researchers are pioneering models to predict how often a stock will be traded and at what price the following day, based on patterns from social media. A trading strategy that's based on the researchers' model "outperformed other baseline strategies by between 1.4 percent and nearly 11 percent and also did better than the Dow Jones Industrial Average during a four-month simulation."[19]

Social media has been targeted by data scientists to use predictive analytics to predict the fluctuating stock market. There are now numerous research papers confirming that the admiration a company gets on social media is a good predictor about stock market performance.

As these sciences evolve further we will find new insights to help us predict future outcomes. According to Dr. Kumar Murty, Chair of the Mathematics Faculty at the University of Toronto:

> large data sets found in social media have interesting mathematic shapes, and advanced mathematics will identify hidden patterns, that traditional methods do not detect easily . . . we have also been partnering with SalesChoice to analyze sales data patterns to help us predict sales forecasts more accurately.[20]

Founder and CEO of SalesChoice, Dr. Cindy Gordon, and her engineering team have developed a powerful predictive analytic engine, partnering with Dr. Kumar's Big Data Research Lab, at the University of Toronto. They have a patent pending technology that will analyze not just the social media patterns correlated to sales cycles, but will also track the customer conversation reach patterns to sales patterns, as they evolve their technology. They will be able to predict at 80 percent or higher predictions, company's sales cycles, odds of closing, leveraging every possible interaction pattern from mobile, e-mail, text, social, sales funnel data, and so forth—bringing advanced insights to sales practices.

We are entering the world where predictive analytics will start to permeate all business processes and practices. Definitely social will be one major area for predictive analytics to play out, but over time there will be a predictive analytic controller connecting all patterns to all patterns.

Sense making will move to another level of performance and human intelligence will simply always be on.

In other words, if you are not hard wiring your company to be smarter in using smarter predictive analytics and have a strategy at the board level, there will be long business growth implications. We also see a strategic requirement to position chief data scientists at a more strategic level versus burying these insights reporting into CIO's or into CFO's roles. Chief data scientists need the mandate to identify and predict any data intelligence risks, irrespective of organizational reporting boundaries. One of the reasons often organizations fail to listen to the future is they are too buried to see it or embrace the possibilities or appreciate the risks. A good example is IBM, which in 2014 is undergoing major restructuring to counter the migration to cloud computing infrastructure, impacting their hardware business. This has been on the outlook for over 10 years with the growth of SaaS. Had there been a chief data scientist with skills in innovation, and predicting risks of future business scenarios, perhaps IBM could have restructured five years prior.

Companies also like SalesChoice have developed incredibly powerful predictive analytics engine to help guide sales representatives on the feasibility of them achieving their quota(s) against the opportunities they are selling. Time is a precious asset. Having insights before they go viral, or assess risk time frames to make changes, will support organizations be more alert, as science starts to enter the board room with advanced intelligence approaches from diverse disciplines, like computing science (artificial intelligence and machine learning), advanced statistics (Bayesian statistics), advanced mathematics (algebraic topology, number theory), sentiment analysis (social network ties); diverse disciplines are fast coming together to create predictive intelligence solutions to integrate into core business processes. The intelligence era is getting that much smarter.

We are rapidly advancing into a new era where it is possible for CEOs to have a new compass. We also believe CEOs of the future will come from stronger advanced sciences and mathematics backgrounds as everything we know in the future will be distilled down into one giant big data and math problem for pattern recognition. There is a good reason why data scientists have moved to being one of the most sought-after talent pools for recruiters to source.

As the world of social interactions continues to mature worldwide, it will soon not be a topic of discussion as it will be simply another mainstream tool to engage in; what will rise will be the wisdom and the insights that can be attributed to the discourse of social. This higher level of performance will be beyond the traditional business intelligence and reporting practices, but rather aggregating all the patterns for more advanced sense making will be required.

In closing, our prediction is social media solutions as we know them today will be acquired and integrated into mainstream or emerging enterprise solution players, like IBM, Oracle, Microsoft, Google and so forth, as the costs of all these separate social solutions, will soon be passé, as consumers and customers recognize the ROI will be on integrated practices, with advanced sense making from predictive analytics permeating everything. In the meantime, the market is still rapidly experimenting with many fragmented approaches, reduced the value of seeing the real patterns at play, or emerging. This is where the rise of predictive analytics will manifest itself. We are not that far away from Siri being everywhere, or Skynet as intelligence will start to permeate everything we know; which is *why big data and predictive analytics are truly the next big thing.*

Discovery Questions

1. What social media metrics does your company use to advance its social media ROI desired outcomes? What is working or not working?
2. Which companies are best in class in social media analytics that your industry can learn from?
3. Do you have a strategy for predictive analytics and how it is emerging?
4. Do you have a chief data scientist in your company? Does your board of director(s) have a chief data scientist officer role?
5. In your role and in your team's role, do you have a social strategy to improve your personal or team's practices, to influence your stakeholder groups(s) or your sphere(s) of influence?

CHAPTER 12

What's Next?

When we started to research this book, it was with the vision that the Social Era was creating giants and social tribes impacting all forms of media channels. The business conversations that were playing out in the early stages of social media usage were more about collaboration behaviors (trust, reciprocity, etc.), value and benefits (return on investment or contribution), and also the concerns (employee productivity loss, attention risks, etc.). Today, the conversations are less about questioning the value of social media usage, rather we are moving forward rapidly into a world of social connected, alertness, where social connections will eventually be everywhere and in all things.

The world is simply becoming flatter, and incredibly interconnected, where all our interactions and social engagement footprints are leaving breadcrumbs along the way. Our anonymity is no longer a reality, despite what privacy laws attempt to do; once we put content on the Web, it is now publically accessible for mining new pathways for reach-out conversations. Our world is social on so many dimensions as illustrated in our social tribe stories. Yet despite the stories we have told, they are merely a glimmer of the changes that we experience in the next 100 years. They will come faster than the past 20 years, and most of us are unaware of the new social intelligence layer(s) that are being created. We think Google has made a difference to the world of search. It has, but the world we are now going to enter will be 1000-fold more intelligent. Let's briefly reflect on the iconic contributions of the early social tribe warriors, before looking ahead at the social intelligence that we envision will be here before we know it.

- Facebook has created the richest consumer mining social
  platform in the world, allowing advertisers to engage in
  customer conversations to test product ideas, or to simply

tracking your friend's activities in the world where everyone is always socially on.

- Twitter has created the shortest microblogging channel (140 characters) bite-sized communication that now carries news faster than any other formal publishing source. Everyone is now in the social media business; each tweet creates an insight to analyze, monitor, or predict what is going viral or trending in advance of the outcome.

- YouTube has allowed everyone to further extend their media reach, allowing stars to be found, educate the masses for free, presell products or services, enable entertainment venues, provide comments on content, and so forth. Video usage from mobile devices being uploaded on to YouTube, now also fights crime. Anyone can create and now produce content in video channels, creating a world that is far more visually demanding.

- Blogger has allowed everyone to become a journalist using low-cost tools to get content out to relevant audiences to spark new conversations in the socially always-connected universe. More people today are reading blogs than traditional newspaper venues, further challenging traditional publishing industries that are not going fully digital.

- LinkedIn has become the business professional's best friend to access relevant contacts, join interest groups, or build personal brand profile. Originally designed to help recruiter's source talent, the company is innovating developing sales tools, marketing advertising to leverage its rich contact directory.

We also touched on the up and comers that are now taking social approaches and integrating social into mainstream business processes impacting learning (CoursePeer), and social selling (realSociable), and social analytics (HootSuite), and also hinting at market players like SalesChoice, who are developing predictive analytics (powerful engines) that can become the nest for analyzing all business process interaction patters, as Siri moves to everyone context and SkyNet starts to become a potential reality with sensors in everything.

We have created a social informed world that expects customer service questions answered in less than 1 minute on a social channel posting.[1] Social always on customer service is now the new telephone.

We thought a fun way to conclude our book was to take a futurist approach telling a story of how we see the world unfolding over the next 10 years, more on the behaviors and interactions of life and business with social always being turned on. We encourage you to send an email to Dr. Cindy Gordon at cindy@saleschoice.com to tell your futuristic stories as part of our ongoing research. Dr. Gordon, principal author of this book, plans to write something very new and different, a fictional story versus nonfiction. We had the Hunger Games, then Divergent, now we will have a Trilogy story in 2015, Sensor World, where social intelligence is simply in sensors everywhere. The following is an extract from her new book that we thought was a fitting conclusion to our new book Social Roots.

Sensor World

It is 9 pm, and Jessica Gordon is out for an evening jog in Central Park. Her Nike runners are calculating her footpace. A small GPS in her glasses signals her to run to the right, as a smart sensor picks up a signal that her best friend Ben is running two blocks in front of her.

Jessica makes a quick comment, "Heh Ben, I can meet you at the nearest café on Broadview at Ideal Café."

Ben responds "Sounds great."

Ideal Café picks up the conversation signals and automatically checks their profile for coffee orders, and seating pattern preferences, and based on their distance an order is queued for immediate servicing.

As Jessica nears the intersection, she looks up to see the smart billboard responds with *Hi Jessica, there is a sale down at 5th Avenue, on Stuart Weitzman's Diamond Dream Stilettos.* An automatic text is sent to her sales shoe file on her smart home portfolio for future reference.

As Jessica and Ben approach Ideal Café, their sensors send a final confirmation to pour their coffees, so by the time they arrive, and sit down at their favorite table, their coffees are already served, and an automatic debit is taken from Jessica's bank account and a short confirmation appears on her iPhone.

Ben and Jessica have been business colleagues at Google for over five years. They love working there as the culture is always turned on to new ways of thinking and working. After coffee, Jessica and Ben quickly signal for an automated taxi to take them to their respective apartments. There are no taxi drivers in New York City anymore. They were phased out due to electric taxi innovations over the past 20 years, with environmental programs.

As they are riding home, they both quickly put their ear phones on to watch two separate channels which have captured reruns earlier in the day of their favorite TV shows. Jessica chooses an historical rerun of The Wolf on Wall Street; Leonardo DeCaprio passed away nearly 50 years ago at the age of 120. An incoming phone call from Jessica's mom appears on the screen, asking how her day was. She also informs Jessica that her blood test results just taken from her recently purchased smart appliances had already confirmed that everything was OK. This good news brightens Jessica's day, as she loves her mother so very much.

Getting to Ben's street, he jumps out and waves Jessica goodbye.

Now with only two blocks to get to Jessica's home, her GPS nest picks up signaling that she will arrive in less than five minutes, the lights go on, and a soothing jazz music starts to play. Her robotic dog, Geniobo moves to be closer to the door, wagging his black and white tail, to greet her. Soothing aromatic scents and herbal essences are released designed to destress and create a calming effect. The lights also softly dim a little more as Jessica's pulse rate is now picked up by the smart walls as she enters her condo unit. As Jessica presses the elevator to the 12th floor, the door automatically opens and greets her.

Harold, the elevator's name, quickly decodes and scans what Jessica is wearing and says, "Jessica how was your run this morning, lovely day for an outing."

Jessica responds, "Yes Harold, it sure was."

As she approaches her condo unit, a smart eye scanner checks her eyes as she is walking to the door and then automatically opens the door for her. Geniobo immediately does a short bark, cocks his ear, wags his tail, and then sits on his hind legs waiting for a stroke. Bending over, Jessica strokes his back side, and Geniobo immediately flops onto his flat smooth tummy kicking his hind legs, hoping for more strokes. Geniobo is given one last tail squeeze, and Jessica breaks out into a broad smile. The smart lights brighten a little more, sensing her body rhythm is relaxing more.

Jessica immediately goes to the fridge and finds a cold mango protein shake prepared for her just 30 minutes ago. As she scans the fridge, Andrew, her fridge, starts to ask what would you like for dinner, "We have available in the freezer, a lasagna dish, a chicken dish and a veal dish, any preferences for us to prepare. There are lots of fresh greens as grocery on the go serviced us this morning for our weekly stock run, so all the eggs are nicely in order by age sequence, and all fruits stacked by organic grade."

"Thanks Andrew for the run down. I think I would like to eat the chicken dish, and I would like a small green salad prepared," comments Jessica.

Like clockwork, Carol, the robot chef comes around the corner: "Did I hear you wanted a salad Jessica, be ready in 15 minutes with your chicken dinner, I have already drawn a bath for you, just the way you like it; see you in fifteen. If you would like company for dinner tonight, I would be delighted to tell you the highlights of the global developments while you are also eating."

"Thank you Carol", responds Jessica. "I would like that."

In the meantime, SIRA is collecting all the statistics for the day profiling Jessica's activities, her wake up time, vital statistics, calories of consumption, food products by brand and amount consumed, music she listened to, and who she spoke to about what topics, and an immediate profile is date stamped and loaded into the Global SIRA Memory Bank. The different brands immediately see their daily product consumption ratings, and use these early predictive analytic indicators to preorder inventory order runs to help sequence and balance out global consumption rates.

A local florist, also close to Jessica's mom's home, sends over a lovely yellow rose with a card, wishing her a bright and sunny day, knowing a smile from their brand will go a long way, as she is a frequent customer picking up flowers often on her way home.

As Jessica steps out of the bath, the floor tiles, her towels, and bath robe have all been warmed for her, so as she steps out, there is only comfort and a sense of peace surround around her. Breathing a sigh, Jessica is then automatically air misted with jasmine oils.

Putting on a lululemon comfy PJ set, and her slippers that Genioba has thoughtfully placed at her bed, she heads to the kitchen, where her chicken parmigiana dish and salad are thoughtfully waiting for her.

Carol is sitting there at the table, patting Genioba's head. "Refreshed?" Carol asks.

"Yes, I feel much better. Dinner smells amazing. I am famished", says Jessica. "So Carol, what are the global developments?"

Carol starts in with an expression of absolute delight, as she loves financial and economic highlights. "Well, let's start with the China's recent developments, a large kitchen wall immediately lights up with a map of China. China has just announced its full continent wide transportation system allowing sky scooters to go coast to coast, this puts China in the leading position in sky transit."

Pictures of the smart scooter sky stations are profiled in quick clips on the screen to give Jessica immediate context.

Continuing on Carol says: "Now let's take a quick snapshot of India. They have just finished their new medical hospital under the Indian Ocean covering over two miles of radius to create the most advanced operating intelligence system. . . . In North America, the GoodCoin currency developed by Dr. Ron Dembo continues to surge in value on the social sustainability stock exchange and GoodCoin is now the #1 social currency in the world. If you recall BitCoin was invented over 50 years ago, and inspirations of GoodCoin were rooted in the pioneering efforts of BitCoin."

They are interrupted by an incoming call from Jessica's brother, Bryce calling in from Sweden. The screen immediately shows Bryce in his home surroundings. "Thought I would check in as I know tomorrow is your birthday; how wonderful to be turning 30 Jessica. Just five years behind you," he grins. "So any special wishes?"

"Nope—I thought I would head over to see Mom though."

"So when are you coming back to visit?"

" Actually I was thinking of taking Rocket Airlines over tomorrow, be there in less than two hours. How does that sound, to join you and Mom for your 30th? Surely it is great now travelling at supersonic transportation warp speeds. Did you hear about the Super Sonic Bullet Airlines opening up? They are promising flight travel to and fro in less than an hour travel time, mind you we have to travel in sedates capsules, but who cares. It makes no difference if I work in New York then and live in Sweden."

"Wow that is so cool. I had not heard about the Super Sonic Bullet Airlines. It will be so amazing to see you Bryce, I can hardly wait, and I know Mom will be so thrilled to bits," responds Jessica.

"See you tomorrow at your time 5 PM, after you get off work," says Bryce.

"It will be grand seeing you Bryce—I have missed you so much," smiles Jessica. With a quick wave, Bryce's image slowly fades off the screen.

"Now that's fun news for you," says Carol, "it has been awhile since Bryce has flown home. With the congestion in air transportation these days, it is wonderful he is able to make it home."

"Sure is", says Jessica, "Now where were we?"

Just before Carol responds, the screen highlights Dalia, the Founder and CEO of realSociable, and behind her image are thousands of networks appearing behind her, flowing blond curly hair, like an eerie extension of hair locks, showing everyone she knows by persona so her life's connections are visible to the world. Her expansive science and thinking created the world's most powerful social connection network enabling all connections to be visible to all, pending permission settings. She was awarded the Nobel Prize recently as well for her social innovation efforts.

"Hi Jessica, I wanted to connect with you on your NEST research on how the advanced sensor chip run is coming along. Going live with the NESTER chip with its genetic implant at birth will be an incredible development to allow us to finally track every human(s), or nonhuman(s) location, so the smart buildings can easily track daily activities to feed Siri automatically. We have already had incredible results with the inanimate object trials tracking their locations with advanced location intelligence tracking over the past 20 years, so this next step is a giant step for human civilization. This will help us further in our social connectivity research, seeing all the social connections made daily in what place, and understanding what purchases were made, to form a more accurate and intelligent understanding of human interactions. Such richness of knowledge in real time is really quite remarkable," says Dalia.

Jessica chimes up enthusiastically, "Yes Dalia, you are right; we are finally entering the Social Intelligence Everywhere Era. Who would have thought that just from the early pioneers from Facebook, Twitter, YouTube, over 50 years ago, could have propelled us into the collective intelligence where smarter connections are in everything. Remember that funny phrase, 'The Internet of things,' at the time it seemed to make a lot of sense, what it did not represent is that the Internet was not the only smart highway for transmitting social intelligence. Sensors Everywhere is the new order. I really love the fact that my running shoes are talking to my socks and when my pads are thinning, new socks arrive at my doorstep, all bases on wearable sensing technology innovations. It is also funny when I check my washing machine(s) reading that the socks life is ending and to limit the amount of bleach being added to increase their wearability. Life sure is different. How generations survived without extra sensory social intelligence is really an interesting question."

"But what I really would like is your help Dalia in helping me key in a few words with your new smarter social dating service," says Jessica.

Giggling, they both brainstorm a number of key attributes: socially outgoing, tall, smart, engaging, loves robotic dogs, enjoys space travel, and deep ocean diving, likes science, and is a foodie are a few of the phrases that Jessica and Dalia key in.

"Good Fun, isn't Jessica," Dalia says, "Don't forget to check his social circle profile to see how many of your connections know of him, and get his social behavior rating from his networks on his values health reading, you never can be too safe these days."

Carol, chimes in, "I will get this information ready for your review for your bedtime review. I have already ordered this request and it will be on your bed's headboard, prior to lights out tonight."

Jessica says, "I am so fortunate to have such good friends like you both, Dalia and Carol."

Genioba hears the word friend and saunters over to the table to get another gentle back rub.

Conclusion

Our world has always had community and social at its core. As technology innovation continues, we will find social context and social relevance moves into societal context at all layers, as our world increasingly becomes smarter. With advanced sensor technologies moving into all objects rapidly, and advanced social consumer solutions evolving, the world has increasingly become much smaller. As intelligent agents permeate everything, social patterns of everything will become more apparent. At the root of this change will always be a primal reality that we are no longer one, we are simply one of the many, but we will be able to choose our social tribes and social networks at a heartbeat, and change our social ecosystems, at a keystroke, or simply a voice command.

Social will simply be everywhere!

Notes

Preface

1. Plato Quote

Chapter 1

1. Constine (2011).
2. Gates (2008).
3. Stone (2011).
4. Brasel and Gips (2011).
5. Tofler (1970).

Chapter 2

1. "Facebook Management" (2014).
2. "Facebook Inc Financials" (2014).
3. "Facebook Inc Financials" (2014).
4. "Facebook Market Cap" (2014).
5. "Facebook.com Site Info" (2014).
6. "Key Facts" (2014).
7. Hoffman (2008).
8. The Crimson Staff (2003).
9. The Crimson Staff (2003).
10. O'Brien (2007).
11. Hoffman (2008).
12. O'Brien (2007).
13. Hoffman (2008).
14. Hoffman (2008).
15. Hempel (2009).
16. Smith (2013).
17. Teller (2006).
18. Teller (2006).
19. Smith (2013).
20. Levey (2011).

21. Morgenstern (2010).
22. Cyran (2011).
23. Cyran (2011).
24. Swisher (2013a, 2013b).
25. Rose (2013).
26. Pew Research Center (2013).
27. Pew Research Center (2013).
28. Smith (2007).
29. Facebook Statistics Brain (2014).
30. Lorber (2014).
31. Hempel (2009).
32. Davies (2012).

Chapter 3

1. "Twitter Executive Team" (2014).
2. "Twitter Inc Financials" (2014).
3. "Twitter Inc Financials" (2014).
4. "Twitter Market Cap" (2014).
5. "Twitter.com Site Info" (2014).
6. "About Twitter" (2014).
7. Parr (2011).
8. Murphy (2014).
9. Murphy (2014).
10. Lennon (2009).
11. Lennon (2009).
12. Kafka (2009).
13. Kafka (2009).
14. Sagolla (2009).
15. Sagolla (2009).
16. Arrington (2006).
17. Lennon (2009).
18. Levy (2007).
19. Douglas (2007).
20. Racoma (2007).
21. Lennon (2009).
22. Stone (2008).
23. Swisher (2008).
24. Arrington (2009).
25. Gaudin (2009).
26. Community (2011), p. 102.

27. Ostrow (2009).
28. Bullas (2011).
29. "Twitter Statistics" (2014).
30. Stone (2008).
31. Veiszadeh (2009).
32. MacAskill (2009).
33. Kiley (2008).
34. Bratt (2009).
35. Bratt (2009).
36. Dougherty (2013).
37. Curtis (2013).
38. Miller (2009).
39. Miller (2009).
40. Johnson (2010).
41. Stone (2010).
42. Parrack (2010).
43. Kessler (2012).
44. Stoll (2012).
45. Johnson (2010).

Chapter 4

1. "LinkedIn Management" (2014).
2. "LinkedIn Corp Financials" (2014).
3. "LinkedIn Corp Financials" (2014).
4. "LinkedIn Market Cap" (2014).
5. "LinkedIn.com Site Info" (2014).
6. "About LinkedIn" (2014).
7. The genesis of this chapter is an unpublished executive primer Watts et al. (n.d.).
8. Householder (2012).
9. Householder (2012).
10. Householder (2012).
11. Yeung (2013).
12. Yeung (2013).
13. Zeevi (2013).
14. Zeevi (2013).
15. Zeevi (2013).
16. Yeung (2013).
17. LinkedIn (2013).
18. Sprung (2012).

19. Anders (2012).
20. Wagner (2013a).
21. Clatterbuck (2013).
22. Gunelius (2012).
23. Buckley (2012).
24. Duermyer (n.d.).
25. How LinkedIn Broke Through (2009).
26. Duermyer (n.d.).

Chapter 5

1. "Myspace.com Site Info" (2014).
2. Angwin (2009).
3. Lapinski (2006).
4. Angwin (2009), Lapinski (2006).
5. Angwin (2009).
6. Lapinski (2006).
7. Sellers (2006).
8. Angwin (2009).
9. Angwin (2009).
10. Angwin (2009).
11. Angwin (2009).
12. Lapinski (2006).
13. Greenspan (2005).
14. Garrahan (2011).
15. Scott (2005).
16. Sabbagh (2010).
17. Garrahan (2011).
18. Garrahan (2009).
19. Halliday (2011).
20. Specific Media (2011).
21. Sellers (2006).

Chapter 6

1. "Wordpress.com Site Info" (2014).
2. "Wordpress.org Site Info" (2014).
3. "About WordPress" (2009).
4. "WordPress' Matt Mullenweg" (2014).
5. Singh (2010).
6. Singh (2010).

7. This Week In Startups (2010).
8. This Week In Startups (2010).
9. This Week In Startups (2010).
10. This Week In Startups (2010).
11. "About WordPress Foundation" (2011).
12. Cubrilovic (2008).
13. This Week In Startups (2010).
14. This Week In Startups (2010).
15. Mullenweg (2013).
16. Mullenweg (2013).
17. This Week In Startups (2010).

Chapter 7

1. UCTelevision (2012).
2. UCTelevision (2012).
3. Livingston (2008), p. 112.
4. Livingston (2008), p. 113.
5. Livingston (2008), p. 113.
6. Livingston (2008), p. 113.
7. Livingston (2008), p. 113.
8. Livingston (2008), p. 114.
9. Livingston (2008), p. 114.
10. Livingston (2008), p. 114.
11. Livingston (2008), p. 115.
12. Quoted in Livingston (2008), p. 115.
13. Quoted in Kim (2010).
14. Kim (2010).
15. Livingston (2008), p. 116.
16. Livingston (2008), p. 116.
17. Livingston (2008), p. 117.
18. Livingston (2008), p. 117.
19. Livingston (2008), p. 118.
20. Hourihan (2001).
21. Livingston (2008), p. 119.
22. Hourihan (2001).
23. Livingston (2008), p. 120.
24. Hourihan (2001).
25. Williams (2003).
26. Williams (2003).
27. Williams (2003).

28. Wikipedia (2009).
29. Olsen (2003).
30. Williams (2003).
31. Williams (2003).

Chapter 8

1. "YouTube Site Info" (2014).
2. "YouTube Statistics" (2014).
3. Karim (2007).
4. Thomas and Buch (2007).
5. Siglin, Tim (2007).
6. Sateo (2006).
7. Thomas and Buch (2007).
8. Edelhauser (2006).
9. Karim (2007).
10. Thomas and Buch (2007).
11. Edelhauser (2006).
12. Hurley (2006).
13. Thomas and Buch (2007).
14. Schonfeld (2011).
15. Sperounes (2007).
16. Maney (2007).
17. Becker et al. (2006).
18. Futuresource Consulting (2011).
19. Becker et al. (2006).
20. Deloitte (2014).

Chapter 9

1. Bandera (1963).
2. Vygotsky (1978).
3. Vygotsky (1978).
4. Bandura (1971).
5. Bingham and Connor (2010).
6. ICQ (1996).
7. MSN Messenger (1999).
8. Bingham and Connor (2010).
9. Wikimedia Quarto (2004).
10. Leuf and Cunningham (2010).

11. Park (2013).
12. Watson and Watson (2012).
13. Bailey (1993).
14. The American Society for Training and Development (2005).
15. Attwell (2008).

Chapter 10

1. This chapter was written by Dalia Astabadi, CEO, realSociable and Dr. Cindy Gordon, CEO SalesChoice Inc.
2. Curtis and Giamanco (2010).
3. Bosworth (1994).
4. Iyar and Gordon (2007) and Gordon (2011).
5. Bosworth (1994).
6. Pramik (2000).
7. Brinker (2012).
8. Davenport (2001).
9. Woods (2008).
10. Ciarallo (2013).
11. Ciarallo (2013).
12. Hague (2007).
13. Gordon (2014).

Chapter 11

1. Schmidt (1996).
2. Crumb (2012).
3. Enge (2007).
4. Roque (2013).
5. Clifton (2009).
6. Clifton (2009).
7. Clifton (2009).
8. Clifton (2009).
9. Regan (2005).
10. Clifton (2009).
11. Lewis (2008).
12. Shorty Award (2011).
13. Shorty Awards (2011).
14. Cohen (2012).
15. Cohen (2012).

16. Hootsuite Enterprise (2012).
17. Gordon (2014).
18. Harold (2012).
19. Harold (2012).
20. Murty (2014).

References

About LinkedIn. 2014. *About LinkedIn,* http://press.linkedin.com/about/ (accessed February 8, 2014).

About Twitter. 2014. *About Twitter,* https://about.twitter.com/company (accessed February 8, 2014).

About WordPress Foundation. 2011. *About WordPress Foundation,* http://wordpressfoundation.org/about/ (accessed February 8, 2014).

About WordPress. 2009. *About WordPress,* http://wordpress.org/about/ (accessed February 8, 2014).

Anders, G. 2012. *How LinkedIn has Turned Your Resume into a Cash Machine,* http://www.forbes.com/sites/georgeanders/2012/06/27/how-linkedin-strategy/ (accessed February 8, 2014).

Angwin, J. 2009. *Stealing Myspace.* New York, NY : Random House.

Arrington, M. 2009. *In Our Inbox: Hundreds of Confidential Twitter Documents,* http://techcrunch.com/2009/07/14/in-our-inbox-hundreds-of-confidential-twitter-documents/ (accessed March 9, 2014).

Arrington, M. 2006. *Odeo Bought Back From Investors,* http://techcrunch.com/2006/10/25/odeo-bought-back-from-investors/ (accessed March 9, 2014).

Attwell, G. 2008. *Web 2.0, Personal Learning Environments and the future of schooling,* http://www.pontydysgu.org/wp-content/uploads/2008/02/web2andfutureofschooling.pdf (accessed January 11, 2014).

Baer, Linda (2014). *Learning and Analytics,* http://www.learninganalytics.net/?page_id=50

Bailey, G.D. 1993. Wanted: A Road Map for Understanding Integrated Learning Systems. In *Computer-based Integrated Learning Systems,* ed. G.D. Bailey, 3–9. Englewood Cliffs, NJ: Educational Technology Publications.

Bandura, A. 1971. *Social Learning Theory.* New York, NY: General Learning Press.

Becker, A., B. Grossman, J.M. Higgins, and A. Rom. 2006. *How the Google-YouTube Deal Shakes up TV,* http://www.broadcastingcable.com/news/news-articles/how-google-youtube-deal-shakes-tv/81179 (accessed February 8, 2014).

Bingham, T., and L.C. Marcia. 2010. *The New Social Learning a Guide to Transforming Organizations Through Social Media.* Alexandria, VA: ASTD Press.

Bosworth, Michael. 1994. *Solution Selling: Creating Buyers in Difficult Selling Markets,* New York, NY: McGraw-Hill.

Brasel, S.A., and J. Gips. 2011. "Media Multitasking Behaviour: Concurrent Television and Computer Usage." *Cyberpsychology, Behavior, and Social Networkding* 14, no. 9, pp. 527–534.

Bratt, E. 2009. *Twitter Success Stories*, http://www.marketingprofs.com/store/product/21/twitter-success-stories (accessed February 8, 2014).

Brinker, Scott. "Conversion Optimization Is The New SEO". April 2012.

Buckley, Z. 2012. *Get LinkedIn or Get Left Out: Using LinkedIn Effectively*, http://www.socialfish.org/2012/08/get-linkedin-or-get-left-out-using-linkedin-effectively (accessed February 8, 2014).

Bullas, J. March 15, 2011. *Twitter Reveals It's Latest Growth Numbers*, http://www.jeffbullas.com/2011/03/15/twitter-reveals-its-latest-growth-numbers (accessed February 8, 2014).

Ciarallo, Joe. "How Cisco Achieved 281% ROI with Social" Salesforce.com Bloc: http://blogs.salesforce.com/company/2013/08/cisco-social-listening.html August, 2013

Clatterbuck. S. 2013. *Making LinkedIn More Accessible*, http://blog.linkedin.com/2013/05/09/making-linkedin-more-accessible/ (accessed February 8, 2014).

Clifton, Brian. 2009. *Google Analytics – Four years on*, http://www.advanced-web-metrics.com/blog/2009/04/16/google-analytics-fours-years-on/ (accessed February 23, 2014).

Cohen, D. 2012. *HootSuite Announces Integration With Webtrends*, http://allfacebook.com/hootsuite-webtrends-integration_b101071 (accessed 18 March 2014).

Community 102. 2011. *The Social Web: How Different Age Groups Interact Online*, http://www.mediabistro.com/alltwitter/social-web-interaction_b13352 (accessed February 8, 2014).

Constine, J. 2012. *Facebook's S-1 Letter from Zuckerberg Urges Understanding Before Investment*, http://techcrunch.com/2012/02/01/facebook-ipo-letter/ (accessed March 23, 2014).

Crumb, C. 2012. *Urchin Founder Reflects On The Impact Of Urchin And Google Analytics*, http://www.webpronews.com/urchin-founder-reflects-on-the-impact-of-urchin-and-google-analytics-2012-01

Cubrilovic, N. 2008. *WordPress Security Issues Lead to Mass Hacking. Is Your Blog Next?* http://techcrunch.com/2008/06/11/my-blog-was-hacked-is-yours-next-huge-wordpress-security-issues/ (accessed March 9, 2014).

Curtis, S. 2013. *Twitter User Buys Promoted Tweet To Complain About British Airways*, http://www.telegraph.co.uk/technology/twitter/10283117/Twitter-user-buys-promoted-tweet-to-complain-about-British-Airways.html (accessed February 8, 2014).

Cyran, R. 2011. *Delay Takes Shine Off Zynga's IPO*, www.breakingviews.com/delay-takes-shine-off-zinga's-apo/1618648.article (accessed March 9, 2014).

Davenport, T. H., J. G. Harris, and A. K. Kohli. 2001, "How do they know their customers so well?", MIT Sloan Management Review.

Deloitte, 2014. *Deloitte TMT Predictions*, http://www2.deloitte.com/global/en/pages/technology-media-and-telecommunications/articles/tmt-predictions-2014.html (accessed July 4, 2014).

Davies, R. 2012. *Leadership Lessons Facebook's Mark Zuckerberg,* http://www.managementtoday.co.uk/opinion/1131649/leadership-lessons-facebooks-mark-zuckerberg/ (accessed February 8, 2014).

Dougherty, J. 2013. *Six Successfully Innovative Twitter Campaigns,* http://www.vocus.com/blog/innovative-twitter-campaigns/ (accessed February 8, 2014).

Douglas, N. 2007. *Twitter Blows up at SXSW Conference,* http://gawker.com/243634/twitter-blows-up-at-sxsw-conference (accessed February 8, 2014).

Duermyer, R. n.d. *LinkedIn Introduction—How Does Linkedin Work?* http://homebusiness.about.com/od/linkedin/a/how-does-linkedin-work.htm (accessed February 8, 2014).

Edelhauser, K. 2006. *Watching YouTube.* http://www.entrepreneur.com/article/168764 (accessed February 8, 2014).

Enge, Eric. 2007. *Interview of Google Analytics' Brett Crosby,* http://www.stonetemple.com/articles/interview-brett-crosby-011207.shtml (accessed 23 February 2013).

Facebook Inc. Financials. 2014. http://www.google.com/finance?q=NASDAQ:FB&fstype=ii (accessed February 8, 2014).

Facebook Management. 2014. http://investor.fb.com/management.cfm (accessed February 8, 2014).

Facebook Market Cap. 2014. http://ycharts.com/companies/FB/market_cap (accessed February 8, 2014).

Facebook Statistics Brain. 2014. http://www.statisticbrain.com/facebook-statistics/

Facebook.com Site Info. 2014. http://www.alexa.com/siteinfo/facebook.com (accessed February 8, 2014).

Futuresource Consulting. 2011. *New Report: Online Video Market Update,* http://web.archive.org/web/20111228062608/http://www.futuresource-consulting.com/report_OnlineVideo.html (accessed February 8, 2014).

Garrahan, M. 2009. *The Rise and Fall of Myspace,* http://www.ft.com/cms/s/0/fd9ffd9c-dee5-11de-adff-00144feab49a.html (accessed February 8, 2014).

Garrahan, M. 2011. *Murdoch's Myspace Dream Turns to Dust,* http://www.ft.com/intl/cms/s/0/9262f82c-a289-11e0-9760-00144feabdc0.html (accessed February 8, 2014).

Gates, B. 2008. Brainy Quotes: http://www.brainyquote.com/quotes/quotes/b/billgates404193.html

Gaudin, S. 2009. *Possible Twitter Lawsuit Would Dive into Murky Blog Waters,* http://www.computerworld.com/s/article/9135606/Possible_Twitter_

lawsuit_would_dive_into_murky_blog_waters (accessed February 8, 2014).

Giamanco, Barbara. 2010. *The New Handshake: Sales Meets Social Media.* Santa Barbara, CA: Praeger.

Gordon, Cindy, 2011. WhitePaper on Collaboration Commerce: Helix Commer Publication.

Gordon, Cindy. 2014. *The Coming Age of Ubiquitous Analytics,* http://www.saleschoice.com/the-coming-age-of-ubiquitous-predictive-analytics/ (accessed February 21, 2014).

Greenspan. 2005. *Free Myspace,* http://web.archive.org/web/20060217193928/ http://www.freemyspace.com/ (accessed February 8, 2014).

Gunelius, S. 2012. *The Complete Idiot's Guide to LinkedIn.* Indianapolis, IN: Alpha Book.

Halliday, J. 2011. *Myspace Rebrand 'Would Have Prevented Its Collapse',* http://www.guardian.co.uk/technology/2011/oct/26/myspace-rebrand-collapse (accessed February 8, 2014).

Harold, Heather. 2012. *Predictive Analytics & Social Media: Predicting the Unpredictable,* http://spotfire.tibco.com/blog/?p=15776 (accessed December 18, 2014).

Hempel, J. 2009. *How Facebook Is Taking Over Our Lives,* http://money.cnn.com/2009/02/16/technology/hempel_facebook.fortune (accessed February 8, 2014).

Hoffman, C. 2008. *The Battle for Facebook,* http://www.rollingstone.com/culture/news/the-battle-for-facebook-20100915 (accessed February 8, 2014).

Hootsuite Enterprise. 2012. *More ways to measure your Social Media ROI with HootSuite Enterprise,* http://socialbusiness.hootsuite.com/webtrends.html (accessed March 18, 2014).

Hourihan, M. 2001. *A Sad Kind of Day,* http://megnut.com/2001/02/a-sad-kind-of-day/ (accessed March 9, 2014).

Householder, K. 2012. *History of LinkedIn,* http://www.cosomedia.com/history-of-linkedin/ (accessed February 8, 2014).

How LinkedIn Broke Through. 2006. http://www.businessweek.com/stories/2006-04-09/how-linkedin-broke-through (accessed February 8, 2014).

Hurley, C. 2007. *You Too,* http://www.forbes.com/forbes/2007/0507/068.html (accessed February 8, 2014).

Iyar, S. Gordon C. 2011. Why Buy The Cow. Boston. WebEx Communications Press/

Johnson, S. 2010. Why We Tweet. In *The Best Technology Writing 2010,* ed. J. Dibbell, 38–49. New Haven, CT: Yale University Press.

Kafka, P. 2009. *Twitter Guys: We'll Still be Running This Company in Five Years,* http://allthingsd.com/20090526/biz-stone-and-evan-williams (accessed February 8, 2014).

Karim, J. 2007. *YouTube: From Concept to Hyper-Growth,* http://dotsub.com/ view/97b35953-1a50-409d-aed8-1636d6e6f309 (accessed February 8, 2014).

Kessler, S. 2012. *Twitter Launches Self-Service Advertising for Small Businesses,* http:// mashable.com/2012/03/26/twitter-small-businesses (accessed February 8, 2014).

Key Facts. 2014. *Newsroom,* http://newsroom.fb.com/Key-Facts (accessed February 8, 2014).

Kiley, D. July, 2008. *Twitter Dominates CMO's Social Network Plans,* http://www. businessweek.com/the_thread/brandnewday/archives/2009/07/twitter_ dominat.html (accessed February 8, 2014).

Kite, Shane. 2011. *Social CRM's a Tough, Worthy Goal,* http://www. americanbanker.com/btn/24_6/social-crm-tough-worthy-goal-1038025-1. html (accessed April 18, 2012).

Kim, H. 2010. *An Interview with Meg Hourihan,* http://lawofsuccess2.blogspot. com/2010/09/interview-with-meg-hourihan_02.html (accessed February 8, 2014).

Lapinski, T. 2006. *Myspace: The business of spam 2.0,* http://gawker.com/199924/ myspace-the-business-of-spam-20-exhaustive-edition (accessed February 8, 2014).

Lamont, Judith. 2012. *Text analytics finds dynamic growth in e-discovery and customer feedback,* http://www.kmworld.com/Articles/Editorial/Features/ Text-analytics-finds-dynamic-growth-in-e-discovery-and-customer-feedback-76365.aspx (accessed February 8, 2014).

Lars-Henrik Schmidt. 1996. Commonness across Cultures. In Anindita Niyogi Balslev (ed.) *Cross-cultural Conversation: Initiation,* ed. Anindita Niyogi Balslev, Oxford University Press, ISBN 0788503081.

Lennon, A. 2009. *A Conversation with Twitter Co-founder Jack Dorsey,* http:// www.thedailyanchor.com/2009/02/12/a-conversation-with-twitter-co-founder-jack-dorsey (accessed February 8, 2014).

LeGresley. 2008. *Invoke Presents Brightkit: The Ultimate Twitter Toolbox,* http:// web.archive.org/web/20081217072144/http://www.invokemedia.com/ invoke-presents-brightkit-%E2%80%93-the-ultimate-twitter-toolbox/ (accessed March 18, 2014)

Leuf, B., and W. Cunningham. 2001. *The Wiki Way: Quick Collaboration on the Web.* Boston: Addison-Wesley.

Levey, A. 2011. *Don't Call It the Next Tech Bubble—Yet,* http://tech.fortune.cnn. com/2011/07/11/dont-call-it-the-next-tech-bubble-yet/ (accessed February 8, 2014).

Levy, S. 2007. *Twitter: Is Brevity the Next Big Thing,* http://www.newsweek.com/ twitter-brevity-next-big-thing-98045 (accessed February 8, 2014).

Lewis Rob. *BrightKit. The Ultimate Twitter ToolBox*, http://www.techvibes.com/blog/brightkit-the-ultimate-twitter-toolbox

LinkedIn Corp Financials. 2014. *Finance*, http://www.google.com/finance?q=NYSE:LNKD&fstype=ii (accessed February 8, 2014).

LinkedIn Management. 2014. http://press.linkedin.com/Management (accessed February 8, 2014).

LinkedIn Market Cap. 2014. http://ycharts.com/companies/LNKD/market_cap (accessed February 8, 2014).

LinkedIn. 2013. http://www.britannica.com/EBchecked/topic/1372553/ (accessed February 8, 2014).

LinkedIn.com Site Info. 2014. http://www.alexa.com/siteinfo/linkedIn.com (accessed February 8, 2014).

Livingston, J. 2008. *Founders at Work*. Berkeley, CA: Apress.

Lorber, A. 2014. *Where are Teens Hanging Out in 2014? Hint: It's Not Facebook*, http://www.forbes.com/sites/gyro/2014/01/09/forbes-where-are-teens-hanging-out-in-2014-hint-its-not-facebook/ (accessed February 8, 2014).

MacAskill, E. 2009. *US Confirms it Asked Twitter to Stay Open to Help Iran Protesters*, http://www.theguardian.com/world/2009/jun/17/obama-iran-twitter (accessed February 8, 2014).

Maney. 2007. Social Media Conference Personal Notes.

Miller, C. July 22, 2009. *Marketing Small Businesses with Twitter*, http://www.nytimes.com/2009/07/23/business/smallbusiness/23twitter.html (accessed March 9, 2014).

Morgenstern, J. 2010. *Last Call for Facebook Gifts*, http://www.facebook.com/notes/facebook/last-call-for-facebook-gifts/405727117130 (accessed February 8, 2014).

Mullenweg, M. 2013. *State of the Word Address*, http://wordpress.tv/2013/07/29/matt-mullenweg-state-of-the-word-2013 (accessed February 8, 2014).

Murphy, P. 2014. *Valuation: Is This Nuts?* http://www.ft.com/cms/s/0/4339f826-7f78-11e3-b6a7-00144feabdc0.html (accessed February 8, 2014).

Murty, Kumar. 2014. Interview with Dr. Cindy Gordon, March 18th, 2014.

Myspace.com Site Info. 2014. http://www.alexa.com/siteinfo/myspace.com (accessed February 8, 2014).

O'Brien, L. 2007. *Poking Facebook*, http://www.informationliberation.com/?id=24402 (accessed February 8, 2014).

Olsen, J. 2003. *Newsmaker: Blog on*, http://news.cnet.com/2008-1025-5094753.html (accessed February 8, 2014).

Ostrow, A. 2009. *Twitter's 1928 Percent Growth and Other Notable Social Media Stats*, http://mashable.com/2009/07/16/twitter-june-2009-growth (accessed February 8, 2014).

Park, B. 2013. *Michael Chasen: Blackboard's Overnight Success in a Span of 15 Years*, http://startupgrind.com/2013/07/michael-chasen-blackboards-overnight-success-in-a-span-15-years/#sthash.X7iz8rAK.dpuf

Parr, B. 2011. *Twitter Now Worth $4 Billion*, http://mashable.com/2011/01/25/ twitter-now-worth-4-billion (accessed February 8, 2014).

Parrack, D. 2010. *Coca Cola Brands 'Promoted Trends' Ad on Twitter a Success*, http://tech.blorge.com/Structure:%20/2010/06/25/coca-cola-brands-promoted-trends-ad-on-twitter-a-success (accessed February 8, 2014).

Pew Research Center. 2013. *Social Networking Trends*, http://www. pewresearch.org/data-trend/media-and-technology/social-networking-use (accessed February 8, 2014).

Plato. Quote: Bartelby Book Quotations. http://www.bartleby.com/348/authors/ 422.html

Pramick. Mike. (2000). Social Media Conference Workshop Personal Notes.

Racoma, J.A. July 28, 2007. *Twitter Gets Funding from Union Square Ventures*. http://www.blogherald.com/2007/07/28/twitter-gets-funding-from-union-square-ventures (accessed February 8, 2014).

Regan, Keith. 2005. *Google Buys Web Analytics Firm Urchin Software*, http:// www.ecommercetimes.com/story/41857.html (accessed February 23, 2014).

Roque, Celine. 2013. *The Real Story on How Google Analytics Got Started*, https:// www.attendly.com/the-real-story-on-how-google-analytics-got-started (accessed February 23, 2014).

Rose, M. 2013. *As EA Bows out Facebook Says Games are as Strong as Ever*, http:// gamasutra.com/view/news/190577/As_EA_bows_out_Facebook_says_ games_are_strong_as_ever.php (accessed February 8, 2014).

Sabbagh, D. 2010. *News Corp Runs out of Patience with Myspace*, http://www. theguardian.com/media/2010/nov/04/news-corp-myspace-losses (accessed February 8, 2014).

Sagolla, D. 2009. *How Twitter Was Born*, http://www.140characters.com/2009/ 01/30/how-twitter-was-born/ (accessed February 8, 2014).

Sateo, S. 2006. *Clip Culture*, http://www.economist.com/node/6863616 (accessed February 8, 2014).

Schmidt, L. 1996. Social Analytics Defined: Wiki Encyclopedia http:// en.wikipedia.org/wiki/Social_analytic

Schonfeld, E. 2011. *Citi: Google's YouTube Revenue Will Pass $1 Billion in 2012 (and so Could Local)*, http://techcrunch.com/2011/03/21/citi-google-local-youtube-1-billion/ (accessed February 8, 2014).

Scott, G. 2005. *Social Networking and Music: Myspace Puts It All Together in a Virtual Community*, http://ezinearticles.com/?Social-Networking-and-Music:-Myspace-Puts-It-All-Together-in-a-Virtual-Community&id=18424 (accessed February 8, 2014).

Sellers, P. 2006. *Myspace Cowboys*, http://money.cnn.com/magazines/fortune/ fortune_archive/2006/09/04/8384727/index.htm (accessed February 8, 2014).

Siglin, Tim. 2007. *Streamticket 2006: The Deals That Reshaped the Online Video Space*, http://www.streamingmedia.com/Articles/ReadArticle.aspx?ArticleID=65164 &PageNum=1 (accessed July 4, 2014).

Shorty Awards. 2011. *Interview with Hoot Suite CEO Ryan Holmes*, https://www.youtube.com/watch?v=ZUUkRQ1TuXg#t=145 (accessed March 18, 2014)

Singh, G. 2010. *Interview with Matt Mullenweg and Mike Little*, http://wordpress.tv/2010/03/09/mullenweg-little-wordpress-interview (accessed February 8, 2014).

Smith, C. 2013. *7 Statistics about Facebook Users That Reveal Why It's Such a Powerful Marketing Platform*, http://www.businessinsider.com/a-primer-on-facebook-demographics-2013-10 (accessed February 8, 2014).

Smith, J. 2007. *Another Facebook App Acquisition Slide Buys Favorite Peeps for $60K*, http://www.insidefacebook.com/2007/06/25/another-facebook-app-acquisition-slide-buys-favorite-peeps-for-60k/ (accessed February 8, 2014).

Specific Media. 2011. *Specific Media Acquires Myspace*, http://specificmedia.com/specific-media-acquires-myspace/ (accessed February 8, 2014).

Sperounes, S. 2007. *Escaping YouTube's Treadmill*, http://www2.canada.com/edmontonjournal/news/culture/story.html?id=4529f9ba-82f3-4066-b4e1-b73352fa251b&k=40748&p=1 (accessed February 8, 2014).

Sprung, S. 2012. *LinkedIn CEO Jeff Weiner Shares Insights on Leadership*, http://www.businessinsider.com/linkedin-ceo-jeff-weiner-talks-about-leadership-2012-9 (accessed February 8, 2014).

Stevens, Howard, and James, Geoffery (2013). The Changing Role of the Sales Professional: from Peddlers to Professionals to Specialists. Chally Group

Stoll, J. 2012. *Twitter Heads to Motown*, http://www.reuters.com/article/2012/04/04/us-twitter-detroit-idUSBRE83311R20120404 (accessed February 8, 2014).

Stone, B. 2008. *Finding a Perfect Match*, https://blog.twitter.com/2008/finding-perfect-match (accessed March 9, 2014).

Stone, B. 2010. *Hello World*, http://blog.twitter.com/2010/04/hello-world.html (accessed February 8, 2014).

Stone, B. 2011. *The Tweets Must Flow*. https://blog.twitter.com/2011/tweets-must-flow (accessed March 23, 2014).

Swisher, K. 2008. *When Twitter Met Facebook: The Acquisition Deal That Fail-Whaled*. http://allthingsd.com/20081124/when-twitter-met-facebook-the-acquisition-deal-that-fail-whaled/ (accessed March 9, 2014)

Swisher, K. 2013a. *Znga Feed*, feed://sanfrancisco.cbslocal.com/tag/zynga/feed/ (accessed January 2013).

Swisher, K. 2013b. *With 1.6B in Cash Zynga Is Now Worth Less Than 750 Million to Investors*, http://allthingsd.com/20130604/with-1-6-billion-in-cash-zynga-is-now-worth-less-than-750-million-to-investors (accessed February 8, 2014).

Teller, S. 2006. *Investors Add $25M to Facebook's Coffers*, http://www.thecrimson. com/article/2006/4/25/investors-add-25m-to-facebooks-coffers   (accessed February 8, 2014).

The American Society for Training & Development. 2005. *A Field Guide to Learning Management Systems*, http://cgit.nutn.edu.tw:8080/cgit/PPTDL../ hclin_091104025632.PDF (accessed January 11, 2014).

The Crimson Staff. 2004. *Facing Off Over the Facebook*, http://www.thecrimson. com/article/2004/9/15/facing-off-over-the-facebook-theres (accessed February 8, 2014).

This Week In Startups. 2010. *This Week in Startups—Matt Mullenweg, Founding Developer of Wordpress*, http://www.youtube.com/watch?v=SP7B0oWTR3o (accessed February 8, 2014).

Thomas, D., and V. Buch. 2007. *YouTube Case Study: Widget Marketing Comes of Age*, http://web.archive.org/web/20070322163029/http://www.startup-review.com/blog/youtube-case-study-widget-marketing-comes-of-age.php (accessed February 8, 2014).

Thompson, Bob. 2009. *Can You Hear Me Now? Top Five Voice of Customer Pitfalls*, http://www.customerthink.com/article/can_you_hear_me_now_top_five_ voice_of_customer_pitfalls (accessed April 18, 2012).

Tofler, A. 1970. *Future Shock*. New York, NY: Random House.

Twitter Executive Team. 2014. https://about.twitter.com/company/leadership (accessed February 8, 2014).

Twitter Inc Financials. 2014. http://www.google.com/finance?q=NYSE% 3ATWTR&fstype=ii (accessed February 8, 2014).

Twitter Market Cap. 2014. http://ycharts.com/companies/TWTR/market_cap (accessed February 8, 2014).

Twitter Statistics. 2014. http://www.statisticbrain.com/twitter-statistics (accessed February 8, 2014).

Twitter.com Site Info. 2014. http://www.alexa.com/siteinfo/twitter.com (accessed February 8, 2014).

UCTelevision. December 1, 2012. *The Atlantic Meets the Pacific: Exploring Technology with Evan Williams*. http://www.youtube.com/watch?v= kTKHgxyH9tA (accessed February 8, 2014).

Veiszadeh, E. June 16, 2009. *Twitter Freedom's Only Link in Iran*, http://www. theaustralian.com.au/news/twitter-freedoms-only-link-in-iran/story-e6frg 6n6-1225736033533 (accessed June 26, 2009).

Vygotsky, L.S. 1978. *Mind in Society: The Development of Higher Psychological Processes*. Cambridge, MA: Harvard University Press.

Watson, W., and S. Watson. 2007. "An Argument for Clarity: What are Learning Management Systems, What are They Not, and What Should They Become?" *TechTrends* 51, no. 2, pp. 28–34.

Watts, C., Gillespie, P., Sand, D., and Terrell, F. *(2013) LinkedIn: A Tool for the Modern Age, unpublished student paper.*

Wikimedia Quarto. 2004. *Interview: Ward Cunningham,* http://wikimedia foundation.org/wiki/Interview/Ward_Cunningham (accessed March 27, 2014).

Wikipedia. 2009. *Pyra Labs,* http://en.wikipedia.org/wiki/Pyra_Labs (accessed March 9, 2014).

Williams, E. 2003. *Bloogleplications,* http://evhead.com/2003/02/bloogleplications.asp (accessed February 8, 2014).

Wordpress.com Site Info. 2014. http://www.alexa.com/siteinfo/wordpress.com (accessed February 8, 2014).

Wordpress.org Site Info. 2014. http://www.alexa.com/siteinfo/wordpress.org (accessed February 8, 2014).

WordPress' Matt Mullenweg. 2009. http://revision3.com/bestof/tekzilla-92 (accessed February 8, 2014).

Yeung, K. 2013. *LinkedIn Is 10 Years Old Today: Here's the Story of How It Changed the Way We Work,* http://www.thenextweb.com/insider/2013/05/06/linkedin-10-years-Social-Network/ (accessed February 8, 2014).

YouTube Site Info. 2014. http://www.alexa.com/siteinfo/youtube.com (accessed February 8, 2014).

YouTube Statistics. 2014. https://www.youtube.com/yt/press/statistics.html (accessed February 8, 2014).

Zeevi, D. 2013. *The History of LinkedIn: A Brief 10 Year Celebration,* http://dashburst.com/linkedin-history-interactive-infographic (accessed February 8, 2014).

Index

DIGITAL AND SOCIAL MEDIA MARKETING AND ADVERTISING COLLECTION HAS MANY FORTHCOMING TITLES, INCLUDING...

Vicky Crittenden, Babson College, Editor

- *Digital and Social Media Marketing: Keeping it Real* by Nathalie Collins
- *Online Consumer Insight* by Geraldine Rosa Henderson
- *Corporate Branding in Facebook Fan Pages: Ideas for Improving Your Brand Value* by Eliane Pereira Zamath Brito
- *Mobile Marketing: A Plan For Strategic Success* by J. Barry Dickinson
- *Mobile Marketing Strategies:* by Karen Mishra
- *Information Privacy in the Marketplace Perspectives on the Information Exchange Between Consumers and Marketers* by George Milne
- *Digital Consumption and Fantasy Football: Lessons For Marketers From America's 'Virtual' Pass Time* by Mujde Yuksel
- *Mobile Commerce: How It Contrasts, Challenges and Enhances Electronic Commerce* by Esther Swilley
- *Electronic Word of Mouth for Service Businesses* by Linda W. Lee
- *Digital Marketing Management: A Handbook for the Current (or Future) CEO* by Debra Zahay
- *Mobile Advertising: Moving from SMS to Mobile Applications* by Aikaterini C. Valvi
- *Presentation Evaluation: How to Inspire, Educate, and Entertain Your Audience* by Michael Weiss
- *M-Powering Marketing in a Mobile World* by Syagnik Banerjee
- *Using and Managing Online Communities* by Edward Boon

Announcing the Business Expert Press Digital Library

Concise E-books Business Students Need
for Classroom and Research

This book can also be purchased in an e-book collection by your library as
- a one-time purchase,
- that is owned forever,
- allows for simultaneous readers,
- has no restrictions on printing, and
- can be downloaded as PDFs from within the library community.

Our digital library collections are a great solution to beat the rising cost of textbooks. E-books can be loaded into their course management systems or onto students' e-book readers.

The **Business Expert Press** digital libraries are very affordable, with no obligation to buy in future years. For more information, please visit **www.businessexpertpress.com/librarians**. To set up a trial in the United States, please email **sales@businessexpertpress.com**.

www.ingramcontent.com/pod-product-compliance
Lightning Source LLC
Chambersburg PA
CBHW050117210326
41519CB00015BA/3994